Insight into IELTS Extra

with Answers

Vanessa Jakeman and Clare McDowell

CAMBRIDGE
UNIVERSITY PRESS

CAMBRIDGE UNIVERSITY PRESS
Cambridge, New York, Melbourne, Madrid, Cape Town, Singapore, São Paulo, Delhi

Cambridge University Press
The Edinburgh Building, Cambridge CB2 8RU, UK

www.cambridge.org
Information on this title: www.cambridge.org/9780521009492

First published 2003
7th printing 2007

Printed in the United Kingdom at the University Press, Cambridge

A catalogue record for this publication is available from the British Library

ISBN 978-0-521-00949-2 Workbook with answers
ISBN 978-0-521-00947-8 Workbook
ISBN 978-0-521-00950-8 Workbook Cassette
ISBN 978-0-521-01148-8 Student's Book with answers
ISBN 978-0-521-62660-6 Cassette

Contents

INTRODUCTION   5

THE LISTENING MODULE

UNIT 1   Orientating yourself to the text   6

Match pictures to context – role of speakers
Anticipating the speakers' questions and relationship
IELTS Section 1 task

UNIT 2   Listening for specific information   9

Multiple-choice type questions
IELTS Section 1 task
Note completion – notes and full sentence format
IELTS Section 1 task

UNIT 3   Identifying detail   13

Focus on facts, figures and details – taking notes
Expanding written notes into talks
IELTS Section 2 task

UNIT 4   Identifying main ideas   17

Listening to short dialogues – identifying speakers and topic
Table completion
IELTS Section 2 task

UNIT 5   Seeing beyond the surface meaning   20

Listening to short conversations
Identifying topic and number of speakers
Listening for opinion – agreeing and disagreeing
Picking the topic from the introduction
IELTS Section 3 task

UNIT 6   Following signpost words   23

Predicting what's coming
IELTS Section 3 task
Focus on signpost words

UNIT 7   Being aware of stress, rhythm and intonation   26

Focus on prosodic features in lectures and talks
Note taking
Intonation in questions
IELTS Section 4 task

THE READING MODULE

UNIT 1   Orientating yourself to the text   30

Recognising the topic and main idea
Summarising main ideas
Recognising key vocabulary
Looking at word formation

UNIT 2   Skimming/scanning for specific information and detail   34

Locating specific information
IELTS tasks

UNIT 3   Identifying main and supporting ideas   38

Recognising linking words – jumbled paragraphs
Types of multiple-choice questions
IELTS task
Linking ideas

UNIT 4   Improving global reading skills   43

Paragraph structure
Topic sentence and key vocabulary
IELTS task

UNIT 5   Summarising   48

Understanding paraphrase
IELTS tasks

UNIT 6   Understanding argument   52

Following the line of development
IELTS task
Recognising arguments
IELTS task

UNIT 7   Identifying opinion/attitude and making inferences   55

Scanning for names
Recognising the writer's views
IELTS task

UNIT 8   The General Training module – Section 1   60

Recognising text types
IELTS tasks

UNIT 9   The General Training module – Section 2   63

IELTS tasks

THE WRITING MODULE

UNIT 1 Describing facts and figures 67
Getting the facts right
Being precise
Describing the data
Approaching the task – 1

UNIT 2 Describing trends 72
Increasing and decreasing trends
Describing stability and fluctuation
Approaching the task – 2
Language focus

UNIT 3 Summarising data 75
Describing significant details
Paragraph structure and links
IELTS Task 1

UNIT 4 Describing a process 80
Studying the diagram
Using appropriate linkers
Organising information logically
IELTS Task 1

UNIT 5 General Training, Task 1 84
Understanding the task
Deciding what to include
Organising the points
IELTS Task 1

UNIT 6 General Training, Task 1 87
Getting your message across
Reasons for writing a letter
Setting the right tone
IELTS Task 1

UNIT 7 Academic and General Training, Task 2 90
Analysing the task
Forming ideas

UNIT 8 Planning a structure 93
Presenting ideas
The body, introduction and conclusion
IELTS Task 2

UNIT 9 Introducing topics and main ideas 96
Using appropriate structures
Rhetorical questions
Expressing feelings
Improving an answer

UNIT 10 Developing an argument 100
Structuring an argument
Focus on cohesion – using linkers
IELTS Task 2

UNIT 11 Writing your answer 104
More work on cohesion
Complex sentences
Grammar – precise use of adjectives and adverbs

THE SPEAKING MODULE

UNIT 1 Part one – the interview 108
Responding fully and appropriately
Linking ideas
Guided speaking
Sentence stress

UNIT 2 More practice for Part one 112
Ways of answering questions
Opening phrases
Guided speaking – talking about sport

UNIT 3 Part two – the long turn 115
Tackling the topic
Focus on making notes
Model long turns

UNIT 4 More practice for Part two 118
Focus on what the examiner is looking for
Brainstorming ideas
More Part two topics
Giving the talk – checking your performance

UNIT 5 Part three – the two-way discussion 121
How to approach the Part three questions
Ways of beginning your answer
Anticipating the issues – expanding the topic

UNIT 6 More practice for Part three 125
More work on giving opinions
Using adverbs to express an opinion

RECORDING SCRIPT 128

ANSWER KEY 142

ACKNOWLEDGEMENTS 158

4

Introduction

Insight into IELTS Extra offers additional practice material to accompany *Insight into IELTS*. Each unit in this book matches its equivalent unit in *Insight into IELTS* and provides supplementary teaching points and exercises that reinforce the skills covered in the course book units. Like the course book, the material in *Insight into IELTS Extra* is directly linked to the IELTS test. The book is pitched at the same level as *Insight into IELTS*. All the exercises are aimed at developing an awareness of the skills required in the test. In addition, there are many IELTS-type texts and tasks.

HOW SHOULD THIS BOOK BE USED?

Insight into IELTS Extra may be used alongside *Insight into IELTS* course book in class or for homework. However, it may also be studied independently by students working alone to prepare for the IELTS exam. Most of the material can be covered by a student working on their own, although there are exercises that require a 'study partner' in order to be of maximum benefit. Working with a study partner offers opportunities for discussion and reflection, and enables students to build up their skills for the Speaking test.

WHAT ARE THE SPECIAL FEATURES OF THIS BOOK?

- The book contains material on all four IELTS subtests (Reading, Writing, Listening and Speaking) and there are units that cover the General Training Reading and Writing modules.

- The materials are fully up-to-date with the IELTS specifications and there is extra guidance on the revised Speaking test introduced in July 2001.

- Each unit contains information on the test, guidance to students and advice in the form of 'Test tips' for each task.

- The approach encourages students to adopt a more mature, 'academic' use of English through the inclusion of vocabulary building exercises, and through activities which focus on the development and expression of ideas, both written and spoken. In addition, there are exercises to improve accuracy in grammar, coherence and cohesion.

- The 'With Answers' edition includes fully annotated tapescripts, keys and sample/model answers for writing activities.

More information about *Insight into IELTS* and the IELTS exam can be found on pages 5 and 6 of *Insight into IELTS* course book.

Listening

Pre-listening

- Look at the twelve pictures below showing people in different situations.
- Try to imagine what the speakers are talking about.

EXTRACT 1

- Listen to Unit 1 Extract 1. You will hear ten short extracts. As you listen, match the pictures to each extract. There are two pictures you do not need.
- Listen to Extract 1 again. Decide which speaker is asking for information and which one is giving information. Where there is only one speaker, can you say who the speaker is talking to?
- Now listen for a final time and make a note of the key words which helped you to do this task.

Extract	Picture	Asking for information	Giving information	Key words
1	a	Speaker 1	Speaker 2	we're looking for / can you tell us / turn left, turn right
2				
3				
4				
5				
6				
7				
8				
9				
10				

Follow-up

- Choose one of the pictures above and write your own script to match the illustration.
- Read it out loud to your study partner and see if he/she can name the picture you have chosen.

EXTRACT 2

IELTS Listening Section 1	**Table completion**

TEST TIP

In Section one you will only hear two speakers at any one time, but there may be more than two speakers in the whole piece.

- Look at the table below. What is the topic of the listening text?
- Read the words at the top of each column and turn them into a full question. This will help you to follow the conversations.
- For each question, decide what information you need to listen for, e.g. a type of food.
- How many speakers do you expect to hear?
- Listen to Unit 1 Extract 2 and complete the table.

Questions 11–20

*Complete the table below. Write **NO MORE THAN TWO WORDS** or **USE A SYMBOL** for each answer.*

STUDENT FOOD OUTLET SURVEY				
	Preferred food outlet?	**Type of purchase?**	**Daily expenditure?**	**More food outlets required?** ✓✓ Yes ✗ No ? Undecided
Student 1	Main Building	11	12	13 ......
Student 2	14	Fruit	15	16 ......
Student 3	17	18	19	20 ......

Follow-up

- Imagine you are going to undertake a survey on one of the following topics.

  Use of the school library or Independent Learning Centre
  Out of school activities
  Shopping facilities in the area
  Type of clothes worn
  Use of the Internet

- Think of four different questions you could ask on the topic you have chosen.
- Create a table like the one above and find at least two people to interview.

Listening

UNIT 2 Listening for specific information

There are three types of multiple-choice question used in the IELTS listening. Read the stem at the top of each question carefully to make sure you understand what is required and then read the possible options to see how these vary.

Pre-listening

- What is the difference between questions 1a and b below? Which is easier to follow? Why?
- Read the stem of each question carefully to see what it is asking. Then read the possible answers. This will help you to focus your listening.

EXTRACT 1

- Listen to Unit 2 Extract 1 and answer question 1.

Circle the correct letter A–C.

1a Susan is looking for a
   A flat of her own.
   B cheap hotel.
   C share house.

1b What kind of accommodation does Susan want?
   A a flat of her own
   B a cheap hotel
   C a share house

Pre-listening

- What is the difference in question format between questions 2 and 3 on page 10?
- What do you think is the most likely context of each question?
- When you read the stem, underline any key words which help you to understand exactly what to listen for.

EXTRACT 2

- Listen to Extract 2 and circle the correct letter A–C.
- Were you tempted to choose any of the 'wrong' answers in Q 1, 2 and 3? If so, why?
- What were the key words on the tape that led you to the correct answer?

TEST TIP

Don't just match words on the question paper to what you hear on the tape. Read the 'stem' of the question carefully to avoid being drawn to the wrong answer.

2 Which lecture did the man attend in the afternoon?

  A psychology
  B sociology
  C history

3 The woman wants to study

  A medicine.
  B medical science.
  C vet science.

EXTRACT 3

Another type of multiple-choice question requires you to choose words from a list.

- Read question 4. Then listen to Unit 2 Extract 3 and answer the question. You have to choose two words here, but you will only get one mark as this is considered to be one question.

- Listen again, and make a note of the exact words used in the recording. Were they the same words as the words in the list?

Question 4

*Circle **TWO** letters **A–G**.*

*Which **TWO** things should they take on the walk?*

  A rucksack
  B water container
  C soft drinks
  D cold food
  E insect repellent
  F camera
  G sunglasses

EXTRACT 4

IELTS Listening Section 1	**Multiple choice**

TEST TIP

There is always an example at the beginning of Section 1.

Questions 5–11

*Circle the correct letters **A–C**.*

Example The students are going on a

  A geography picnic.
  B sports club trip.
  C university outing.

5 The coach leaves the bus station at

  A 7.00 am.
  B 7.45 am.
  C 8.00 am.

6 The journey there will take approximately
  A 2 hours.
  B 2 and a half hours.
  C 3 hours.

7 Maria doesn't have the information because she has
  A recently joined the university.
  B been away on holiday.
  C changed her course.

8 The first activity will be to
  A walk across the top of the dam.
  B view the dam from downstream.
  C see the dam in operation.

9 The students will sleep in
  A cheap accommodation.
  B overnight cabins.
  C tents.

10 Meals will be provided in the form of
  A breakfast only.
  B breakfast and lunch.
  C breakfast and dinner.

11 Sydney's daily water consumption is equal to the contents of
  A 20,000 kms of pipes.
  B 600 full-size swimming pools.
  C 262 service reservoirs.

Questions 12–14

*Which **THREE** things does Steve recommend bringing?*

*Circle **THREE** letters A–F.*

  A binoculars
  B camera
  C penknife
  D map
  E raincoat
  F mobile phone

> There are two basic forms of note completion task in *IELTS* listening.
> Type 1: Prompts are given in note form, not in full sentences.
> Type 2: Prompts are given in the form of sentences which you must complete using up to three words. Sometimes the missing words come in the middle of the sentence, but more often they come at the end.

Pre-listening

- Look at the note completion tasks below. Which type of note completion is each question? Write 1 or 2 in the second column.

- Which of the two formats do you find easier to follow when listening. Why?

- Turn the prompts below into full questions, and decide what type of information you must listen out for. Write a note about this in the third column.

		Type 1 or Type 2 ?	Type of information needed
Example: Bus departs at			
What time does the bus depart?		Type 1	A time
15 The man wants to study .... at university.			
16 Louis Pasteur was born in .... (2 possible questions.)			
17 Cost of concession ticket $			
18 Address .... Street			
19 Reason for delay			
20 New Yorkers consume .... gallons of water each day.			
21 Date of arrival			
22 The problem of longitude plagued the early navigators for years because they lacked the ability to			
23 Type of car			
24 Spring rolls are made from			

EXTRACT 5

IELTS Listening Section 1	**Note completion**

- Look at the task below. What do you think the context of the listening will be?
- Turn the notes in the task into a full question, e.g. When is the conference?
- Write a note in the column on the right about what you expect to hear, e.g. *a number, place.*
- Now listen to Unit 2, Extract 5 and complete the task.

Questions 25–34

*Complete the notes below. Write **NO MORE THAN THREE WORDS** for each answer.*

		Type of information needed
<u>Architecture 21 conference</u>		
Conference <u>dates</u>	**(25)**	....
Conference <u>venue</u>	**(26)**	....
Reservations ~~phone no.~~	**(27)**	....
Cost $300 for 3 days		
Student rate $150 for 3 days or	**(28)** .... a day	....
Contact <u>person</u>	**(29)**	....
<u>Must act fast!</u>		
Closing date for talks	**(30)**	....
Send outline to include	**(31)**	....
maximum length	**(32)**	....
Also send	**(33)**	....
e-mail address	**(34)** .... @uniconf.edu.au	....

Listening

Pre-listening

- Look at the ideas below.
- Write questions to find out this information about the game of football (soccer).

First football leagues?

World famous football clubs?

Rules of the game?

Origins of the game?

History of the World Cup?

Most famous player ever?

EXTRACT 1

- Listen to five mini-talks on different aspects of the game of football. Match the talks to the topics in the thought bubbles on page 13. Write the topic in the topic column in the table below.

- Listen again and note down important details. Don't write full sentences.

- Now spend about 10 minutes trying to turn your notes back into complete sentences so that they could be read and understood by somebody else.

Talk	Topic	Details
1		
2	mo,t famou player	the achia he hasmde
3	rule o teagme	
4		
5		

FIFA (handwritten, left margin)

Asking for details

- Working with your study partner, take it in turns to ask each other the questions you wrote at the beginning of this unit. Answer from your notes.

- You can also ask new questions based on your notes. Ask about details.

Further practice

- Work with your study partner. Each choose one of the two topics below and put into a logical or chronological order.

- Write full sentences to make a short talk about the topic.

- Then write some notes with four or five pieces of information missing to give to your study partner.

- Take it in turns to read out your talk and complete the notes.

Germany – School to train dogs started after WWI to help blind soldiers.

1928 Young American (blind) went to Switzerland to train. Returned to USA with dog 'Buddy'. Guide dog HQ opened in New Jersey.

1931 First Guide Dog Centre in Britain.

1927 Article in New York newspaper on German dog-training program

1819 – Vienna Institute for the Blind founded – guide dogs trained, but work unknown internationally.

1952 Training centre opened in Perth, Australia.

1940 McDonald brothers Maurice and Richard set up their first hamburger restaurant in San Bernadino, California.

1948 Closed the business — re-opened with no service, but offering cheap food.

1950 The brothers advertised "1 million burgers sold".

1954 The brothers sold out to Ray Kroc — bought the business and the name.

1937 McDonald brothers' opened drive-in restaurant — no hamburgers sold.

1952 US magazine did a story on the brothers' success and first franchise opened in Phoenix.

Pre-listening

Summary completion is similar to note completion, but instead of short phrases, you have to complete sentences or paragraphs. Read the summary carefully before you start, to get a sense of what it is about.

▶ Ask yourself these questions.
Do you play chess or any other board games?
What do you know about the game of chess?
Have you ever wondered where the game originated?

EXTRACT 2

IELTS Listening Section 2	Summary completion

- For each question, decide what sort of information you should listen for.
- Try making questions to ask about this information,
  e.g. *How old is the game of chess?*
- Make a note in the margin of what type of information
  you expect to hear, e.g. *a date*.
- Now listen to Unit 3, Extract 2 and complete the task.

Questions 6–15

*Complete the notes below. Write **NO MORE THAN THREE WORDS** for each answer.*

The Origins of Chess	Type of information
○ Chess originated in either Afghanistan or **6** .... around the year AD 600. However, the game might even be **7** .... years old.	....
○ There is international agreement on the **8** .... but some variations exist e.g. in Japan and **9**	....
○ The variety played in Europe and America came from Iran and was established in Italy and Spain around the year AD 1000. The Vikings took it to Scandinavia and it had reached Central Europe by **10** AD .... using the present day rules.	....
○ The **11** .... used today in championships originated in the 19th century and were named after an English chess champion.	....
○ First official championships took place in 1866 in London. To avoid running overtime, they used a **12**	....
○ The winner was from Bohemia – in effect the first **13** .... He held the record until 1894 when he was beaten by a German born American who was then beaten by a Cuban named Jose Capablanca. Some people rank Capablanca among the **14** .... who ever lived.	....
○ Also in this league was Bobby Fischer – the first **15** .... to become World Chess Champion.	....

Listening

UNIT 4 Identifying main ideas

 EXTRACT 1

- You will hear ten short dialogues.
- Listen to Unit 4 Extract 1 and decide who the speakers are and where they are. Complete the first two columns of the table as you listen.
- Listen again and identify the topic and purpose of the conversation. Complete the third column.

Conversation	Speakers?	Where are they?	Topic or purpose of conversation?
1 *Example*	Shop assistant and customer	in clothes shop	Assistant attempting to make a sale
2			
3			
4			
5			
6			
7			
8			
9			
10			

- Listen again and this time listen for the phrasal verbs used in the dialogues. Make a note of them and try to work out what each verb means, e.g. in number 1, *to try on* means 'to put clothes on to see if they fit'.

The IELTS listening test may include a table to complete with information you hear. This information is often listed in a logical sequence or in a pattern and so understanding this pattern will help you to complete the task correctly. Read all the information given in the table carefully before you listen so that you can predict the type of information you need to listen for.

Pre-listening

- Read the information given in the tables. What is the topic of each table?
- From the words given, work out what kind of information you will need to complete each table.

a

Zoo animal	Food consumed in captivity
Panda	bamboo
Orang Utan	....
....	hens' eggs
Zebra	....

TEST TIP

Sometimes, parts of the table are shaded to show that you will not hear any information about this.

b

Name of navigator	Country of origin	Famous for discovery of
Columbus	....	America
Magellan	Portugal	....
Marco Polo	....	
....	England	....

c

HISTORY OF HOT AIR BALLOONING			
Date	**Balloon created by**	**Means of propulsion**	**Significance**
1783	Montgolfier brothers	....	First recorded flight
1783	Charles	hydrogen	....
....	Yost	high altitude gas	First new generation hot air balloon
1960		....	Prototype modern hot-air balloon

EXTRACT 2

IELTS Listening Section 2	Mixed question types

In Section 2 you will always hear one person giving a talk on a topic of general interest.

- Read questions 11–20. What do you think the context of this extract is?
- How many different types of question can you identify?
- For each question decide what sort of information is needed: main idea or detail?

Question 11

Choose the correct letter A–C.

11 At the start of the talk, the announcer says that canoeing is
   A safer than people think.
   B usually enjoyable.
   C becoming more popular.

Questions 12–18

*Complete the notes below. Write **NO MORE THAN THREE WORDS** for each answer.*

White-water canoeing

- Type of river: 12 ....

Types of race	
13 take .... between points	e.g. *runner*
steer between 14	e.g. 15 ....

- Recommended areas in Britain 16 .... and ....

Equipment	
Canoe	Pay between 17 £ .... and ....
Helmet	
18	*for beginners*

Questions 19–20

Choose the correct letter A–C.

19 Cynthia says that when you first try canoeing, you should
   A avoid graded rivers.
   B choose something like a canal.
   C take someone experienced with you.

20 According to Cynthia, serious canoeists
   A take risks on purpose.
   B prefer to teach people in the winter.
   C know when a river is too dangerous.

Follow-up

- Listen again to Extract 2. Make a note of all the phrasal verbs you hear on the tape and make sure you can explain their meaning within the context of the talk.

- Try writing some *short* dialogues to illustrate the meaning of six of the phrasal verbs you found in either Extract 1 or 2.

Listening

 EXTRACT 1

- Listen to Unit 5, Extract 1. You will hear ten short conversations. Complete the table below, with information about the topic, number of speakers and whether they agree with each other or not.

	Topic	No. of speakers	Do they agree?	Expression used to agree or disagree
Example	cinema/movies	2	Yes	I thought the music was great. I thought so too.
1				
2				
3				
4				
5				
6				
7				
8				
9				
10				

- Now listen to the conversations again, and this time write down the expression(s) used by the speakers to give their opinions.
- Where the speakers do not agree with each other, are they expressing a strong opinion, or politely disagreeing with each other? Listen again and notice how the speakers use expressions and intonation.

EXTRACT 2

Following a conversation

At the beginning of section 3, there will usually be an introduction to the topic. If you identify it right at the beginning, it will help you to understand the conversation better.

TEST TIP

Take note of any sound effects or music that you hear, as this has been included to help set the scene.

- In Extract 2, you will hear five different introductions A, B, C, D and E.
- Listen to Unit 5 Extract 2 and answer the following questions for each one.

Introduction	A	B	C	D	E
Where are the speakers?					
How many speakers are there?					
What is the topic?					

 EXTRACT 3

IELTS Listening Section 3	Mixed question types

In Section 3 you will hear a discussion between two or more speakers who will be giving information, expressing opinions or saying how they feel about something. The topic will be of an academic nature or possibly related to a course of study.

- In Extract 3 you will hear one of the introductions again, followed by the complete text.
- Look at questions 11–14 below before you listen, to see what information you need to listen out for.
- How many different question types are there? Have you met them before?
- Now listen to Unit 5 Extract 3 and answer the questions.

Questions 11–14

*Write **NO MORE THAN THREE WORDS** and/or **A NUMBER** for each answer.*

11 How does John describe the land his father bought? ....

12 How long did it take to change? ....

13 What was the cause of the problem? ....

14 What did people believe to be the problem? ....

Questions 15–20

Choose the correct letter A–C.

15 John chose South Australia for his sanctuary because

    A they were slow to change the law.

    B it still had many native animals.

    C environmentalists were welcomed.

16 John was put in jail because he

    A was outspoken about the environment.

    B wanted to kill cats and foxes.

    C cut down some trees.

17 John signed the agreement because he

    A was sorry for what he had done.

    B thought the document was worthless.

    C wanted to get out of jail.

18 The woman student suggests you can protect endangered animals by

    A doing research.

    B writing articles.

    C raising money.

19 The male student believes

    A introduced animals are a pest.

    B all animals have a right to live.

    C Watson's views are wrong.

20 Ultimately, John's approach is based on

    A reason.

    B science.

    C emotion.

Follow-up

Sometimes, we don't use language with its exact meaning. We say something, usually with a special emphasis, but mean the exact opposite. This is called 'irony'.

- Listen to Unit 5 Extract 3 again and listen for any language which could be described as ironic, where the speaker is using language beyond the surface meaning.

- Can you explain how you understood the speaker's intended meaning?

Listening

UNIT 6 Following signpost words

Signpost words help us to predict what direction a conversation or talk is going in, because they point us towards the next idea.

Pre-listening

- Look at the words and phrases in the centre of the page and decide what kind of information might follow, e.g. a contradiction, an example, an additional piece of information.

- Complete each of the speech bubbles with the most appropriate word or phrase.

 EXTRACT 1

- Now listen to Unit 6, Extract 1 and check your answers. Pay particular attention to the intonation used by the speakers.

- Try using these signpost words to express some of your own ideas.

a .... I told her not to bother, my friend insisted on driving me to the airport.

b .... , we now have to worry about my sick grandmother too.

c .... , before we go, I'd just like to thank you all for coming along to the meeting this evening.

On top of everything else
Even though
Inspite of
Secondly
Besides
For example
Finally
No matter what
Not only
Nevertheless
As a result of

People always think that foreign languages are spoken much faster than their own language. .... , they say 'Don't New Yorkers speak fast!' but, in reality, it's just a problem of understanding.

d .... you do, you can't avoid growing older each year, but, for your own sake, you can at least try to stay fit.

e .... the burglary, we have decided to put bars on the windows.

f .... is the new law going to make it more expensive to smoke cigarettes, it's also going to discourage young people from taking it up in the first place – which has to be a good thing.

Pre-listening

▶ Ask yourself these questions.

What do you know about the International Space Station (ISS)?

Would you like to spend 90 days in space with 6 other people? Why? Why not?

What kind of things would you have to prepare yourself for?

What advice would you give to anyone who was going?

 EXTRACT 2

IELTS Listening Section 3	Multiple choice / Table completion

- Read questions 1–3 below and then listen to the first part of Unit 6 Extract 2 and answer them.

- Listen carefully for any signpost words.

Questions 1–3

Choose the correct letter A–C.

1 How many nations are involved in the ISS?

  A 5

  B 15

  C 20

2 How much should the ISS have cost to build?

  A $ 8 billion

  B $ 120 billion

  C $ 128 billion

3 How is the water supply maintained on board?

  A by recycling all the water

  B by using very little

  C by transporting plenty from Earth

- Now look carefully at questions 4–10 before you listen to the second part of Extract 2.

- Work out exactly what kind of information you need to listen out for.

Questions 4–6

*Which **THREE** areas of research will take place on the ISS?*

*Choose **THREE** letters A–G.*

A solar energy
B plant cultivation
C mapping
D weather patterns
E studies in weightlessness
F psychology
G nutrition

Questions 7–8

*Which **TWO** things do all the astronauts do each day?*

*Choose **TWO** letters A– F.*

A turn on the computers
B cook breakfast
C attend meetings
D listen to CDs
E take physical exercise
F communicate with family

Questions 9–10

*Complete the table below. Write **NO MORE THAN THREE WORDS** for each answer.*

Date	Details
1998	'Unity' and 'Zarya' modules launched and (9) ....
1999	Tonnes of equipment delivered.
2000	Supply module attached, providing air, water, (10) .... and ....
2006	Estimated date of completion.

TEST TIP
The words and dates in the table act as anchors to guide you, so listen carefully for these words.

Follow-up

• Listen to Extract 2 again and make a note of all the signpost words you hear. Can you say what kind of information they introduce?

Listening

In Section 4 of the IELTS listening test you will hear a talk or a lecture. Recognising the intonation patterns and listening for the signpost words will help you to understand what you hear.

Pre-listening

- Look at the extracts below, which are the opening paragraphs of lectures on different topics. Read them to yourself and decide what the topic is for each, e.g. biography, astronomy.
- Underline the words you think should be stressed and show where your voice should rise and fall.
- Look for signpost words that may help the listener anticipate the meaning. Make sure you emphasise these when you read them.
- Now read the extracts out loud, as if *you* were giving the lecture.

 ## EXTRACT 1

- Listen to the recordings in Unit 7 Extract 1 and compare them to your version.
- If you can, record your own voice and listen to yourself.

a
Heat always tends to move from places where there is a lot of heat to places where there is not quite so much. The transfer of heat from one place to another can be brought about in three ways, namely conduction, convection and radiation.

b
How intelligent are you? It's a question psychologists often ask, but now two mathematicians argue that it's meaningless. They say their experiments with computer 'mini-brains' prove that intelligence depends on the environment and can't exist independently of it. The work has reignited a fierce debate on the nature of intelligence.

c
Who were the first astronomers?
Humans have always looked to the sky, trying to understand the celestial bodies that sweep across it. The ancient Greeks were the first to record their observations, and apply them to calculate the size of Earth and its relativity to the Moon and the Sun. Then, in the second century AD, Ptolemy concluded that Earth was the centre of the universe, a philosophy generally accepted for 1500 years.

d
We all have our image of the Amazon. For some it's a romantic place where the world's greatest river, its largest rainforest and its most diverse ecosystems coexist in harmony. For others, it's a place echoing to the sound of chainsaws, turned to ashes by farmers and defiled by mercury spewing from gold mines.

e A ballad is a narrative poem which tells a story – usually an exciting story – and one which also conveys an idea about the time in which it was written. Ballads date back hundreds of years, to the days when books were rare; and so people would tell stories instead. Many of the first ballads told tales of courage, superstition and mystery.

f It seems that languages have one single purpose – to communicate thought. Nevertheless, this aim is achieved in many different ways. As far as we can tell, there is no aspect of grammar or syntax that is universal or without which we cannot create language.

- The extracts a–f include a number of three- and four-syllable words.

1 Find all these words in the texts and write them in the appropriate column.

2 Is there a rule for the pronunciation of the different spelling patterns? If so, what is it? Make sure you can pronounce them all with the stress on the correct syllable. This will help you to recognise them when you meet them in a listening test.

-tion /shun/	-ology, -ologist	-ent, -ence	Others
conduction	psychologist	intelligent	astronomer

EXTRACT 2

Making your own notes

- You will hear the introduction to a radio programme about Emma Darwin, the wife of Charles Darwin. There are three clear sections to this introduction.

3 As you listen, write down the key words which carry the main meaning. Then think of a suitable heading for each section of the introduction.

	Key words	Main focus
Section 1	Charles worked hard Emma intelligent...	
Section 2		
Section 3		

- How clear were your notes? From the information you wrote down, can you re-construct the three main points the speaker made about Emma Darwin?

EXTRACT 3

Intonation in questions

- Look at these two pairs of questions. What is the difference between the questions in each pair? Which is easier to understand?

a Who was Ptolemy?

Do you know who Ptolemy was?

b When were the pyramids built?

Can you tell me when the pyramids were built?

4 Read the questions out loud. How many different meanings can you make by putting the stress on different words?

Pre-listening

- Read the questions in the task below. What is the topic? How many different types of question are there?

- Look carefully at questions 6–9 to find out exactly what information is required. Remember that a flow chart represents a sequence of events.

 EXTRACT 4

IELTS Listening Section 4	Flow chart and making a list

Question 5

Choose the correct letter A–C.

5 What does the speaker compare a computer virus to?
  A a biological organism
  B a corrupt program
  C an irritating person

Questions 6–9

*Complete the flow chart. Write **NO MORE THAN THREE WORDS** for each answer.*

History of computer viruses

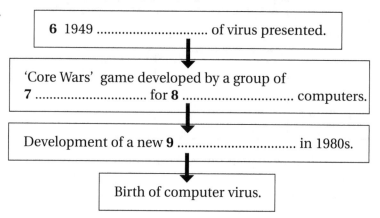

6 1949 .... of virus presented.

↓

'Core Wars' game developed by a group of
7 .... for 8 .... computers.

↓

Development of a new 9 .... in 1980s.

↓

Birth of computer virus.

Question 10

Choose the correct letter A–C.

10 What does the speaker find surprising?
    A the rise in the number of software infections
    B the determination of those who develop viruses
    C the fact that people blame their own computers

Questions 11–14

*List **FOUR** ways of combatting viruses.*

*Write **NO MORE THAN THREE WORDS** for each answer.*

11 ....

12 ....

13 ....

14 ....

 ## EXTRACT 5

IELTS Listening Section 4	**Labelling a diagram**

> Another task you may meet in IELTS is one where you label a drawing from information you hear.

- Look at the diagram representing a solar heating system and work out what parts you will need to label. Then listen to the beginning of a talk about solar energy and complete the task as you listen.

Reading

The title and sub-heading of each reading passage should provide some information about the topic and how it will be developed. You then need to look for the main idea in each paragraph in order to build up an overall understanding of the passage.

RECOGNISE THE TOPIC AND MAIN IDEA

• Read paragraph a below. What are the *topic* and *main idea*?

a Time is one of the fundamental quantities of the physical world, being similar to length and mass in this respect. Three methods of measuring time are in use at present. The first two methods are based on the daily rotation of the earth on its axis. These methods are determined by the apparent motion of the sun in the sky (solar time) and by the apparent motion of the stars in the sky (sidereal time). The third method of measuring time is based on the revolution of the earth around the sun (ephemeris time).

The paragraph is about 'time' so that is the *topic*. The *main idea* concerns methods of measuring time.

1 Read paragraph b and underline the topic and main idea.

b Photographs taken as recently as 30 years ago are already fading in the nation's family albums. Millions of images taken since the invention of modern colour photography are changing because of the way their dyes break down. Just as we now tend to view the 19th century in delicate shades of sepia, there is a fair chance that future generations will look back on the last three decades of the 20th as the era of purple lawns and red skies.

2 What are the two ways of describing the topic in paragraph c? Write the main idea in your own words.

c People are skilled at perceiving the subtle details of human motion. A person can, for example, often recognise friends at a distance purely from their walk. Because of this ability, people have high standards for animations that feature humans. For computer-generated motion to be realistic and compelling, the virtual actors must move with a natural-looking style.

SUMMARISE THE MAIN IDEAS

> As you read through the passage, it is a good idea to make a mental summary of the main ideas, especially as some main ideas are expressed in a number of sentences. This helps you to develop an overview of the whole passage.

- Read paragraph d and underline the topic and main idea.

---

d My parents always encouraged me to play, and I'm sure my childhood experiences are partly why I have been studying animal play for the past 30 years. I realised early on how much could be learned about the behaviour and minds of animals by playing with them and watching them play, but I also discovered that studying play behaviour was easier said than done. Many researchers had tried, but few details were available – trying to understand play was more difficult than they had anticipated. Some even decided that there was no such thing as play or that this muddled area of behaviour could never be unravelled. But gradually, my research and that of others has proved them wrong.

---

3 Which of the following sentences best summarises the main idea?
  A The writer is as confused about the role of animal play as other researchers.
  B The writer's research is helping to explain what animal play involves.
  C The writer has used existing research on animal play to support her own theories.

4 Read paragraphs e–g and write a summary sentence for each one.

---

e Observational equipment has in the past few years been pushed to the limit to identify planets orbiting nearby stars. It has become a popular area for astronomers and one that has attracted some of the most wildly ambitious space projects. One of these is Darwin, a massive super-telescope for the 21st century, 40 times larger than the Hubble Space Telescope. Darwin's objective is to concentrate on Earth-sized planets orbiting 300 sun-like stars, many visible to the naked eye and less than 50 light years away: next door in astronomical terms.

---

f Our sense of humour is truly perplexing. Surveys show we are ten times more likely to be seen sharing a moment of laughter than any other form of strong emotion. Humour saturates our lives, yet only recently have brain scientists started to turn their scanners and electrodes to the task of examining the flash of amused insight that lies at the heart of understanding a joke. And the findings are not at all what you might think.

---

g The very thing that makes the Internet a robust system, capable of surviving lots of random damage, also makes it more susceptible to an intelligent attacker intent on bringing it down. According to a mathematical model published this week, if Internet nodes were to start failing at random, 18 per cent could disappear and most of the Internet would remain connected. But if an intelligent attacker targeted the most important nodes, the network would quickly break into isolated fragments and stop functioning.

---

5 Re-read paragraphs a–g and decide which technique is used to develop the main idea. There may be more than one answer in each case.

    i draws on personal experience
    ii provides an everyday example
    iii predicts some unexpected results
    iv provides statistical data
    v draws a comparison

6 Match paragraph g with one of the headings below.
    A Internet needs to become more powerful
    B Weakness revealed by current research
    C The future, scientists argue, looks better
    D Just one example of what the computer can do

> **TEST TIP**
>
> Some IELTS tasks such as paragraph headings test your understanding of the main ideas in paragraphs.

RECOGNISE KEY VOCABULARY

> You are unlikely to understand all the words in the IELTS reading passages, but this is not necessary to understand the main ideas. However, it is important to recognise which words give you key information.

- Read the paragraph below and underline any words that you do not understand.

> **h** One of the major problems with guidebooks is that they are outdated before they are even published, as it takes on average two years from commissioning to publication. And as the shelf-life of most books is two years, there may be as much as four years between the original research and a tourist's visit. In extreme cases this can have serious repercussions, as a young backpacker, Joel Emond, 18, discovered one autumn. A walk described as non-problematic by one travel guide around a lake near the North Korea border in north-east China resulted in him being arrested by soldiers and imprisoned for a month. The guide has since apologised to him.

> This paragraph contains some difficult words such as 'outdated', 'shelf-life' 'and 'repercussions'. It also contains specialist words about books such as 'published', 'commissioning' and 'publication'.

Look at how the word is formed

> Sometimes it is possible to guess what a difficult word means, for example, 'outdated' is similar to the adjective 'out-of-date'. The two parts of the word 'out' and 'date' also help you understand that this word means 'not current' or 'old-fashioned'.

7 Can you guess the meaning of 'guidebook', 'shelf-life' 'non-problematic' and 'backpacker'?

Read the word in context

> You can also look at the text that comes before and after the word. 'Repercussions' is followed by an example about a backpacker. This example helps you understand that the word means an 'effect' which is often negative.

8 Read the paragraph again and write a summary sentence of it.

Vocabulary builder

- The words and expressions below are taken from paragraphs **a–h**. Which meanings can you guess or work out from the context of the paragraph, and which do you need to look up in a dictionary?

Words	Phrases	Collocations (words often seen together)
a based (on) apparent(ly) **b** fading era **c** feature **d** anticipate(d) unravel(led) **f** saturate(s) **g** robust susceptible (to) targeted **h** outdated backpacker	**a** in this respect **b** look back **d** easier said than done **e** pushed to the limit the naked eye **f** lies at the heart of **g** at random **h** shelf-life	**b** (good/fair) chance **c** (high/low) standards **e** (wildly) ambitious **f** (truly) perplexing → confusing (only) recently **h** (major) problems (serious) repercussions

- Complete the gaps with a *word* from the vocabulary box. You may need to change the form of the word.

9 My last day at school marked the end of an important ...... *era* ...... in my life.

10 The novelist admitted that he had ...... *based* ...... his book on a childhood experience.

11 Young infants are very ...... *susceptible* ...... to catching colds and other common illnesses.

12 Cigarette advertisers should not .... adolescents in their promotion campaigns. *target*

- Complete the gaps with a *phrase* or *collocation* from the vocabulary box.

13 Giving up chocolate is ...... *ambitious* ...... *easier said than done*

14 I put my photographs in the album ...... *at random* ...... so they are a bit muddled.

15 There is a .... that most sportsmen or women will break a bone at some stage in their careers. *good chance*

16 Why anyone would want to work with dangerous animals is ...... *perplexing* ...... *truly*

Reading

In the IELTS test you have an hour to read and answer questions on *three* passages, of approximately 900 words each. Skimming and scanning are important skills you will have to use to answer the questions.

- Before you read the following text for meaning, practise your *scanning* skills by moving your eyes down the lines of the text very quickly in order to find, and underline the following things. Take about 15 seconds for each.

TEST TIP

Sentence completion questions often test factual information like this.

1 a US state *[handwritten: South Carolina]*
2 an American soil researcher *[handwritten: John Sadler]*
3 a company
4 a country other than the US *[handwritten: Israel]*
5 a fruit or vegetable *[handwritten: Tomato]*

Fruitful Drinking

It's what tomatoes everywhere have been thirsting after

A smart irrigation sensor that gives plants only as much to drink as they need can increase tomato yields by more than 40 per cent. The sensor has been developed by Yehoshua Sharon and ben-ami Bravdo at the Hebrew University of Jerusalem's faculty of agriculture in Rehovot, Israel. The researchers say that their system not only increases the yield of crops, but it also dramatically reduces water usage – by up to 60 per cent for some crops.

At the heart of the system is an electronic sensor that clips onto a plant leaf and measures its thickness to an accuracy of 1 micrometre. 'A leaf's thickness is dependent on the amount of water in a plant,' says Sharon. 'A healthy leaf is 60 per cent water.' A thin leaf is a sure sign that the plant is suffering stress because it is thirsty, and stress is bad for yields.

The sensor consists of two plates, one fixed and the other spring-loaded, which together grip the leaf. The moving plate is connected to a small computer that regulates the voltage in an electrical circuit. As the leaf's thickness changes, the plate moves, causing a change in the voltage. This signal is fed to a processor that adjusts the plant's water supply.

Unlike conventional irrigation systems, which water crops periodically, the Israeli system waters the plants continuously, but adjusts the flow to the plant's needs. 'The idea is to give the plant the proper amount of water at the correct time, according to what the plant requires,' says Sharon.

Field studies show the system increases the yields of several crops while reducing consumption of water. Yields of grapefruit increased by 15 per cent while needing 40 per cent less water. For peppers, the yield rose by 5 per cent while water usage fell by 60 per cent. Tomato plants yielded 40 per cent more fruit while consuming 35 per cent less water.

'It is an interesting idea,' says John Sadler, a soil scientist at the US government's Agricultural Research Service in Florence, South Carolina. 'Other researchers have measured stress by measuring a plant's temperature or stem thickness. But I haven't heard of anyone doing irrigation at such a refined level,' he says.

But Sadler is a little surprised by the figures for water savings. 'They would depend on the technique you're comparing these results with,' he says. Sharon says the savings are based on comparisons with the Israeli government's recommendations for irrigating crops.

He admits that the system has to be very reliable if it is to be effective. 'Because the plants are watered continuously they are more susceptible to sudden changes in water supply,' he says. 'This means our system has to operate very reliably.'

The researchers have founded a company called Leafsen to sell the new irrigation system, and they hope to start marketing it within the next few months.

New Scientist

Sometimes scanning skills are used to *locate* a section of the text that contains a number of answers related to a particular topic.

- Look at the diagram below. *Scan* the text on page 34 and circle the written description of the diagram.

LABELLING A DIAGRAM

IELTS Reading

Questions 6–9   7

*Complete the labels on the diagram below. Choose **NO MORE THAN THREE WORDS** from the passage for each answer.*

... **9** ... – controls water supply to plants

process or

... **6** ... used to calculate   ... **7** ... of leaf

sensor   *thickness*

... **8** ... – monitors electrical circuit

small computer

Vocabulary builder

10 *Scan* the text on page 36 and underline the following words and phrases. What do they mean?

- **a** holds the key
- **b** multinational corporations
- **c** vaccines
- **d** solar energy
- **e** developing countries
- **f** tropical diseases
- **g** socially responsible
- **h** take into account
- **i** genetically modified crops
- **j** revolutionise

Time stands still

Simple solutions can transform lives, so what are we waiting for?

IN a world where 2 billion people live in homes that don't have light bulbs, technology holds the key to banishing poverty, says the United Nations in a major report published this week. But rich nations and multinational corporations need to do a lot more to put technology into the hands of the world's poorest people.

Even the simplest technologies can transform lives and save money. Vaccines, crops, computers and sources of solar energy (see Table) can all reduce poverty in developing countries. For example, cheap oral-re-hydration therapy developed in Bangladesh has dramatically cut the death toll from childhood diarrhoea.

But there has been a "market failure to meet the needs of the poor", says lead author Sakiko Fukuda-Parr. "There's no global framework for supporting research and development that addresses the common needs of poor people," she says.

Multinationals must become part of the solution, because they own around 60 per cent of the world's technology. But they seldom make products for poor customers. Of 1223 new drugs marketed worldwide from 1975 to 1996, for example, just 13 were for tropical diseases.

"It's the big corporations that own the technology that really should read this report," says Fukuda-Parr. "We're asking them to be more socially responsible." They could do more to provide vital products such as medicines at different prices around the world to suit what people can afford (*New Scientist*, 7 July, p6). Or pledge a percentage of their profit towards research and development for the poor.

Governments from rich countries should pay more too. They and other sources such as the World Bank and international institutes could provide as much as $10 billion. Developing countries should also make better use of intellectual property laws that entitle them to vital medicines, just as South Africa did recently with AIDS drugs.

Life-changing	
	Vaccines for malaria, HIV and TB
	New varieties of sorghum, assava and maize
	Cheap computers and wireless connections
	Cheap solar and fuel cells for local electricity supplies

Critics of the report say it doesn't take poor people's views into account. "You have to ask: is it affordable to people who earn less than a dollar a day? Is it accessible to them? Can it be managed by local people?" says Lucja Wisniewska of the British-based charity Intermediate Technology Development Group.

Controversially, the report backs genetically modified crops despite the widespread opposition to them among Western environmentalists and non-governmental organisations "To reject it entirely is forgoing a huge opportunity," says Fukuda-Parr. "If it's so good for multinationals, why shouldn't it be used by poor farmers," she says.

Computers could also revolutionise the lives of poor people allowing them to tap into a global wealth of free information that could help solve local problems. But they'd need to be cheap and wireless. Fukuda-Parr says that Brazil and India have already developed cheap computers, proving that countries can do it for themselves.

But the objectives will be difficult to achieve. Time has stood still in sub-Saharan Africa, where there has been no increase in tractor use for a decade. ■

Andy Cochlan

New Scientist

SENTENCE COMPLETION

IELTS Reading

of print letter

Name   Fukada-Parr

Pre-task questions

11 What sort of information are you looking for in order to answer question 16?

12 What type of information do you need to answer questions 15 and 18? *city or number*

13 What are the key words that you should *scan* for in question 19?

14 How does the format of question 21 differ from the others? *South Africa*

Questions 15–21 🕐 13

*Complete the sentences below, which are based on the passage on page 36. Write **NO MORE THAN THREE WORDS** or **A NUMBER** for each answer.*

2 billion

… **(15)** … people in the world still live without domestic electricity.

Fukada-Parr is quoted in … **(16)** … *New Scientist*

More than half the world's technology is owned by … **(17)** … *multi national company*

Between 1975 and 1996 a total of … **(18)** … new drugs were marketed. *1223*

South Africa has recently benefited from referring to … **(19)** … *AIDS drug.*

The writer is surprised to find that the UN report supports the production of … **(20)** … *genetically*

… **(21)** … and … … have produced their own computers. *modified*

Brazil India

In the exercises that you have done so far, scanning skills have been used to locate *facts*. But these skills are also used to locate opinions or arguments as you will see in the coming units.

RHETORICAL QUESTIONS

Rhetorical questions are sometimes used in written texts in order to emphasise a point or argument. They are called 'rhetorical' because they do not require an answer.

• What point is the writer trying to make in these rhetorical questions from the text?

22 Simple solutions can transform lives, so what are we waiting for? (sub-heading)

23 If it's so good for multinationals, why shouldn't it be used by poor farmers? (lines 52–54)

• Try writing three of your own rhetorical question using words or phrases from the vocabulary builder on page 35, e.g.

How socially responsible is it to sell cigarettes to children?

Reading

IELTS reading passages are real texts written for the English-speaking world. The writers give them structure by using paragraphs, words and expressions which help the reader to follow the text. Identifying the links between paragraphs will help you find the difference between the main and supporting ideas.

NOTE HOW IDEAS ARE LINKED TOGETHER

- Use your understanding of linking words and phrases to put the following jumbled paragraphs into the correct order.

a This latest abbreviation has come about because new technology is making it possible to store the text of a book digitally so that it can be downloaded, and printed and bound, one copy at a time.

b Some answer to this problem will have to be found. It's true that while we are still producing books in their present form they will be available as a record of present-day knowledge for the use of future generations. But this is only true for as long as they last physically.

c For if you look a short way into the future, what about works appearing only in electronic form? They are the ones which are most in danger. When we have become totally dependent on electronic devices for the dissemination of information, shall we be able to rely on the publishers of the future to ensure that before an old system becomes totally obsolete all that it stores will be recorded on the newest system?

d Having been stored electronically, you would be able to choose those sections of the material which interest you, and have them printed, leaving out all the sections which you do not need, and do not want to have to carry around with you.

f Not only that, but you may be able to make some books up to suit yourself – for instance, if you were planning a trip, you could put together your own travel guide.

e But putting all the advantages aside, the worrying thing is that the various electronic devices currently used in recording books will sooner or later be superseded by new developments, which will make the current systems out-of-date.

h Given time, the new developments will become obsolete in turn. And so it will continue. Once obsolescence occurs, unless such measures are taken, it may easily become impossible to retrieve the contents of outdated discs. And this may deny our literature, history and technical knowledge to future generations.

g The book trade has used certain abbreviations for many years. OP, for example, stands for Out of Print, meaning that the book is no longer available. TOP means Temporarily Out of Print, which is to say that the publishers have not yet given an order to reprint, and are not quite sure whether they will. Now they have a new abbreviation to learn: POD, which means Print on Demand.

gadfcebh

- Write a title and sub-heading for the article.
- Compare what you have written with your study partner.
- Read the following extract from an article on air travel at the end of the 1990s, and highlight any links that you can find between or within the paragraphs. The first two links have been identified for you.

The sky's the limit

The Economist

Airlines are making money again, but they are also making their growing numbers of passengers miserable. They need to find ways of doing one without the other

Civil aviation is a tale of two contrasting trends: on the one hand, there is strong growth in sales and profits for the world's airlines, on the other, there is increasing misery and dissatisfaction for travelers, especially in America and Europe. For an industry that collectively lost $15 billion in the first few years of the 1990s, the past few years have brought a welcome change. The net profits of all scheduled airlines worldwide rose from $4.5 billion in 1995, when the boom began, to $8.5 billion two years later. However, the airlines are having to work harder and harder for them. The average consumer is paying 70% less per passenger-mile in real terms than 20 years ago, and revenue per seat is declining by an average of 2% per year.

At the same time, consumer dissatisfaction with air travel has reached a new peak in America, as we approach the new century. Hollywood has even started making movies that incorporate the frustrations of air travel in the plot. The prospect of airline mergers is met with even greater hostility. Seeing what a poor job the airlines are doing, the public refuse to believe that bigger will mean better.

Moreover, the airlines are now being attacked by environmentalists for contributing to global warming as well as causing noise pollution around airports.

Although jet engines today are much quieter than they were ten years ago, the huge rise in the number of flights makes the problem more pervasive.

To cap it all, consumer groups are now attacking airlines for squashing in too many people. Sitting still for long periods in cramped conditions, they say, can cause blood clots. In response, some carriers are taking out a few rows of seats to create more space for economy passengers to move around in. But dissatisfaction keeps rising.

Why is the industry failing to keep its customers happy. One answer is that it has been growing so fast, even in a supposedly mature market such as America, that airlines, and the air-transport infrastructure of airports and air-traffic control, have simply not been able to keep up. Although the airlines like to say that 70% of delays are caused by the weather (i.e. not their fault), many of these delays could in fact be avoided or shortened, if the system worked better.

But consumer pressure in response to gridlocked skies is only one force for change in the air travel industry to be faced in the 21st century. Equally important are the parallel trends of privatization and liberalization, which are proving unstoppable....

- Using what you have highlighted to help you, answer these questions:

1 Give an example of a linking word that provides a contrast.

2 What does 'them' (line 19) refer to. What type of link is this?

3 Give an example of a linking phrase that can be used to introduce another main point to an argument *or* to introduce an opposing argument.

4 Give an example of a linking word that is used to add another main point to an argument.

5 Is the sentence about Hollywood a main idea or a supporting point?

6 What function does the word 'even' have in line 29?

7 Find another example of 'even' in paragraph 3. Does this example of 'even' function in the same way as the previous example?

8 Which phrase means 'in addition to all the other bad things that have been mentioned'?

9 Which phrase introduces a positive response to a question?

MULTIPLE CHOICE

In the reading paper, multiple-choice questions take two forms. The stem may be a complete question and you choose from whole sentence answers, e.g. Q13 below, or the stem may be the start of a sentence which you have to complete with one of the sentence endings, e.g. Q14.

IELTS Reading

Pre-task questions

- Read questions 13–17 first and answer the following questions about what sort of information is being tested.

10 Which question asks you to judge the writer's purpose?

11 Which question focuses on a supporting point?

12 Which questions test your understanding of a main idea?

Questions 13–17 🕙 10

Choose the correct letters A–D.

13 What claim is the writer making in the first paragraph?
   A People dislike the huge profits that airlines make.
   B America and Europe have the most profitable air routes.
   C There are positive and negative developments in air travel.
   D There are two approaches to analysing concerns about air travel.

14 According to the writer, the profits that airlines make
  A have consistently grown.
  B fell to their lowest in 1995.
  C cost the consumer more than in the past.
  D are proving increasingly hard to maintain.

15 The writer refers to Hollywood movies in order to illustrate the
  A overwhelming importance of air travel.
  B extent of public frustration with air travel.
  C growth in public involvement in air travel.
  D current financial investment in air travel.

16 Which **THREE** of the following issues are mentioned by the writer?
  A the size of modern airports
  B the worldwide polluting effects of fuel emissions
  C the fact that engines are noisier than they used to be
  D the increasing volume of air traffic
  E the dangers to passenger health
  F the size of aeroplane seats

17 In the sixth paragraph, the writer is
  A making excuses for the airline industry.
  B suggesting reasons for the industry's problems.
  C supporting an earlier argument about the airline industry.
  D outlining solutions to the industry's problems.

• Can you explain why the other options are wrong in each question?

> **TEST TIP**
> Multiple choice questions follow the order of information in the passage.

> **TEST TIP**
> Some multiple choice questions require more than one answer.

LINKING IDEAS

• Use a word or phrase that you have met in this unit to create a link between the pairs of sentences in 18–22. You should not try to make them into one sentence, but you need to make a bridge between them, e.g.

I need to be in the right mood to study.
I find it difficult to study in a room which is not insulated from noise.

I need to be in the right mood to study. Moreover, I find it difficult to study in a room which is not insulated from noise.

18 The publishing industry has recently taken a number of technological leaps forward. The question remains as to whether technology will improve literary content.

19 Computers are widely seen in classrooms today. Children as young as five are learning to use them.

20 The fast food industry faces considerable criticism from health professionals these days. Companies now often claim that their food is nutritious and full of healthy ingredients.

21 We are now in a position to order our groceries over the Internet. We can benefit from the extra leisure time this gives us.

22 It was disappointing that our football club lost in the final on Saturday. It didn't help that the captain tripped over and had to be taken off on a stretcher. Then, the referee gave a penalty kick to the other side as a result of the accident.

Vocabulary builder

- The words and phrases below, which refer to groups of people, appear in the texts in this unit.
- First scan the texts for each word and note line numbers.

23 Using a dictionary to help you, explain the meaning of the words as they are used in the text.

  a future generations

  b publishers

  c airlines

  d passengers

  e travellers *People going on a journey, often to new or foreign places.*

  f the average consumer

  g the public

  h environmentalists

  i customers

TEST TIP

The article on airline travel is American and contains examples of American spelling (e.g. 'travelers'). IELTS accepts both types of spelling in all modules of the test.

Reading

UNIT 4 Improving global reading skills

IELTS reading passages are constructed in different ways depending on whether the main focus is factual, gives information or opinion. Whatever its purpose, the text should have clearly structured paragraphs.

PARAGRAPH STRUCTURE

You have already learned how to identify the main idea or theme of a paragraph by recognising the topic, main ideas and supporting points, and understanding the key vocabulary.

- Read this paragraph and the labels which explain its structure.

comparison to strengthen main idea

topic

David Bordwell is a scholar who writes as a fan. He is in love with the crazy, rip-roaring, vulgar confusion that is Hong Kong Cinema, but he also knows how and why it works and explains it in words the layman can understand. Like American westerns, Hong Kong action movies travel well because their common currency is basic emotions such as fear, anger, joy and sorrow. A theme in many Hong Kong historical movies is a desire for revenge, a universal feeling, while Japanese historical films often turn on the two-way pull of duty and inclination, an idea that is remote for most modern audiences. This is why Bruce Lee's films were hits worldwide but Akira Kurosawa's never reached beyond the art-house circuit.

detailed explanation of main idea

contrast with Japan to further illustrate main idea

specific example given as evidence for main idea

1 Which of these words or phrases is most important to your understanding of the main idea of this paragraph. Can you work out what it means?
   A rip-roaring
   B common currency
   C sorrow
   D layman

2 Which is the most suitable heading for this paragraph?
  A The social importance of Chinese film stars
  B The growing success of Japanese cinema
  C The global attraction of Hong Kong cinema
  D The healthy competition in the film industry

• Complete the labels on the following paragraph.

further information on Teilhard

TEST TIP

The topic or main idea of a paragraph may not come at the beginning.

In the 1930s, the French philosopher Pierre Teilhard de Chardin predicted the emergence of a noosphere, a network linking mankind at the mental rather than the physical level. Teilhard was a sociologist, a scientist and a Jesuit theologian; *he described this noosphere partly in physical terms, as an information network, and partly in spiritual and philosophical language, as a force which would act to unify society. One of the many metaphors which he used to put the concept across was that of a 'halo of thinking energy' encircling the planet.* Today, the same combination of technical, sociological and philosophical terminology is used to describe the Internet.

3 ....
  ....

4 ....

5 ....

• Which words do you not understand?

• Do they prevent you from understanding the main idea?

• Read the passage opposite and answer the following questions:

 6 What is the purpose of paragraph A?

 7 What is the purpose of the fourth and fifth sentences in paragraph B?

 8 Which sentence expresses the main idea in paragraph C?

 9 What theme links paragraphs D, E and F?

10 What are the two main criteria for selecting items for natural history museums?

11 What does 'such collections' refer back to in paragraph H?

12 Write a two or three-sentence summary of the passage, using paragraph I to help you.

Behind the scenes at the museum

The Economist

With more and more of what museums own ending up behind locked doors, curators are hatching plans to widen access to their collections.

A ▶ When, in 1938, the Smithsonian National Museum of Natural History, in Washington, DC, decided it had run out of space, it began transferring part of its collection from the cramped attic and basement rooms where the specimens had been languishing to an out-of-town warehouse. Restoring those specimens to pristine conditions was a monumental task. One member of staff, for example, spent six months doing nothing but gluing the legs back on to crane flies. But 30 million items and seven years later, the job was done.

B ▶ At least for the moment. For the Smithsonian owns 130 million plants, animals, rocks and fossils and that number is growing at 2–3% a year. On an international scale, however, such numbers are not exceptional. The Natural History Museum in London has 80 million specimens. And, in a slightly different scientific context, the Science Museum next door to it has 300,000 objects recording the history of science and technology. Deciding what to do with these huge accumulations of things is becoming a pressing problem. They cannot be thrown away, but only a tiny fraction can be put on display.

C ▶ The huge, invisible collections behind the scenes at science and natural history museums are the result of the dual functions of these institutions. On the one hand, they are places for the public to go and look at things. On the other, they are places of research – and researchers are not interested merely in the big, showy things that curators like to reveal to the public.

D ▶ Blythe House in West London, the Science Museum's principal storage facility, has, as might be expected, cabinets full of early astronomical instruments such as astrolabes and celestial globes. The museum is also custodian to things that are dangerous. It holds a lot of equipment of Sir William Crookes, a 19th century scientist who built the first cathode-ray tubes, experimented with radium and also discovered thallium – an extremely poisonous element. He was a sloppy worker. All his equipment was contaminated with radioactive materials but he worked in an age when nobody knew about the malevolent effects of radioactivity.

E ▶ Neil Brown is the senior curator for classical physics, time and microscopes at the Science Museum. He spends his professional life looking for objects that illustrate some aspect of scientific and technological development. Collections of computers, and domestic appliances such as television sets and washing machines, are growing especially fast. But the rapid pace of technological change, and the volume of new objects, makes it increasingly hard to identify what future generations will regard as significant. There were originally, for example, three different versions of the videocassette recorder and nobody knew at the time, which was going to win. And who, in the 1970s, would have realised the enormous effect the computer would have by the turn of the century?

F ▶ The public is often surprised at the Science Museum's interest in recent objects. Mr Brown says he frequently turns down antique brass and mahogany electrical instruments on the grounds that they already have enough of them, but he is happy to receive objects such as the Atomic domestic coffee maker, and a 114-piece Do-It-Yourself toolkit with canvas case, and a green beer bottle.

G ▶ Natural history museums collect for a different reason. Their accumulations are part of attempts to identify and understand the natural world. Some of the plants and animals they hold are "type specimens". In other words, they are the standard reference unit, like a reference weight or length, for the species in question.

Other specimens are valuable because of their age. One of the most famous demonstrations of natural selection in action was made using museum specimens. A study of moths collected over a long period of time showed that their wings became darker (which made them less visible to insectivorous birds) as the industrial revolution made Britain more polluted.

H ▶ Year after year, the value of such collections quietly and reliably increases, as scientists find uses that would have been unimaginable to those who started them a century or two ago. Genetic analysis, pharmaceutical development, bio-mimetrics (engineering that mimics nature to produce new designs) and bio-diversity mapping are all developments that would have been unimaginable to the museums' founders.

I ▶ But as the collections grow older, they grow bigger. Insects may be small, but there are millions of them and entomologists would like to catalogue every one. And when the reference material is a pair of giraffes or a blue whale, space becomes a problem. That is why museums such as the Smithsonian are increasingly forced to turn to out of town storage facilities. But museums that show the public only a small fraction of their material risk losing the fickle goodwill of governments and the public, which they need to keep running. Hence the determination of so many museums to make their back room collections more widely available.

PARAGRAPH HEADINGS

TEST TIP

Paragraph heading tasks also test your ability to eliminate 'distractor' headings. These are additional headings that are listed in the set but do not correspond to any of the paragraphs in the reading passage.

IELTS Reading

Pre-task questions

13 What is the best way to approach the paragraph heading task?

14 What is the key word in heading vi?

Questions 15–22 ⏱ 15

The reading passage has nine paragraphs A–I.

From the list of headings below, choose the most suitable heading for each paragraph.

List of Headings

i	An unexpected preference for modern items
ii	Two distinct reasons for selection in one type of museum
iii	The growing cost of housing museum exhibits
iv	The growing importance of collections for research purposes
v	The global 'size' of the problem
vi	Why some collections are unsafe
vii	Why not all museums are the same
viii	The need to show as much as possible to visitors
ix	How unexpected items are dealt with
x	The decision-making difficulties of one curator
xi	The two roles of museums
xii	Who owns the museum exhibits?
xiii	A lengthy, but necessary task

Example	*Answer*
Paragraph A	**xiii**

15 Paragraph B

16 Paragraph C

17 Paragraph D

18 Paragraph E

19 Paragraph F

20 Paragraph G

21 Paragraph H

22 Paragraph I

Vocabulary builder

23 Scan paragraphs A–E for noun phrases that have the following meaning.

Meaning	Paragraph	Noun phrase
a big job		
globally		
these large collections		
a difficult task		
a small part		
the two roles		
the main place where things are kept		
his work time		
the fast speed		
people alive in the next 100 years or so		
the year 2000		

Reading

When you read a passage, you can use your skills to note the main ideas in paragraphs and to follow the links and references. In order to do well in IELTS, you also need to be able to understand the IELTS questions. These often include a paraphrase or re-wording of ideas within the passage.

- The following sentences are paraphrases of ideas in the passage below. Read the passage and see if you can find the original wording for each paraphrase. Underline your answers.

1 There are plenty of reasons why chocolate sells well.

2 The human love of chocolate is a global phenomenon.

3 More money is spent marketing chocolate and sweets than any other similar product.

4 Although well-known brands achieve the highest sales, new products are also important.

5 The short-term availability of a 'limited edition' appeals to consumers' desire for a change.

Soft centres – hard profits

•••••••••••••••• Are you being seduced by the sweet industry? ••••••••••••••••

If chocolate were found to be seriously addictive, then the UK would need major therapy to kick the habit. The British
5 lead the world in their love of the cocoa-based treat. As a product, chocolate has a lot going for it, appealing to all ages, both sexes and all
10 income brackets. In 1997, the value of the total UK confectionery market increased by 3% to a staggering £5.2bn, with
15 chocolate sales accounting for 70%, at £3.6bn, and sugar confectionery the remaining £1.6bn.

The UK market has shown consistent growth – increasing over the last decade by around 16%. 20 'Chocolate confectionery is a market that seems to be remarkably resilient', says Pamela Langworthy, marketing for Thorntons, the 25 luxury chocolate producer and retailer. It also increasingly transcends national boundaries. In 1997, Swiss Nestlé, the 30 largest confectioner, exported over a quarter of its production to more than 100 countries. Nestlé has recorded particularly fast growth in confectionery sales in Asia, with the expansion of KitKat into several countries in the region. Eastern Europe provides another promising market. But few markets challenge the UK in terms of current confectionery consumption. In the US, the land associated with excess, each American devours a mere 10kg of confectionery per person a year, whereas UK consumers each manage 16kg. In Europe, where the chocolate market is estimated to be worth over £12bn ($18.5bn), the UK accounts for almost a third of that total, followed some way behind by Germany, France and Italy.

Around 60% of all confectionery is bought on impulse, which makes its availability a key determinant of sales. Impulse buying also makes the development of a strong brand image vital, and large, long-established brands dominate the market. Building up these brands costs serious money. Media expenditure on confectionery exceeds that for any other impulse market. The Cadbury & Trebor Bassett 1997 *Confectionery Review* reveals that in 1996 media expenditure on chocolate reached £94m, compared with £69m spent on soft drinks, £31m on the lottery and £23m on crisps and snacks.

Innovation is also essential for ongoing success, despite the chocolate market being dominated by consistent performers. In 1996 the chocolate company Mars launched 'Flyte', claiming to be the first mainstream brand to address the demand for lower fat products. At 98 calories a bar, Flyte is designed to appeal to weight-conscious women. Another 1997 Mars launch, Celebrations, is claimed by the company's annual review to be showing signs of 'revolutionising the boxed chocolates market by attracting new, younger customers'. 'Traditionally, the boxed chocolates market hasn't changed very much. People who buy the products tend to be older and female. With Celebrations, we are finding that younger people and men are buying because the chocolates don't come in the traditional-shaped box – they look different. Products such as Flyte and Celebrations are attempts to introduce a new product category and increase sales for retailers, rather than just shifting market share,' a Mars spokesman says.

One feature of the chocolate industry in recent years has been the emergence of special editions. The concept of a marketing triumph. Producers believe that special editions offer the consumer a new and exciting variation of a product, while suggesting the same consistent quality they associate with familiar brands. Since special editions are only available for a few weeks while stocks last, they also have a unique quality about them. Far from denting sales of the straight version, limited editions appear to simply boost overall sales.

Accountancy

SUMMARY COMPLETION

This task becomes a little more difficult when the paraphrases are made into a summary paragraph because you will need to follow the structure of the summary. There are two types of summary completion task. The summary below must be completed using words or numbers from the reading passage.

IELTS Reading

Pre-task questions

6 How much of the passage does the summary cover?

7 Is the summary testing ideas or facts?

Questions 8–12 8

Complete the summary below.

*Choose **ONE OR TWO WORDS OR A NUMBER** from the passage for each answer.*

Chocolate – the figures

The chocolate market in the UK in 1997 was worth ... (8) ... , having shown a steady increase during the preceding ten-year period. Overall the manufacturer Swiss Nestlé supplies chocolate to over ... (9) ... and the company has seen rapid growth in the markets in ... (10) ... . Nevertheless, the UK market remains the biggest. Surprisingly, British consumers devour more than their ... (11) ... counterparts and, in terms of the European chocolate market, their consumption amounts to ... (12) ... of the total revenue.

The second type of summary has a box of possible answers. There will always be more than one answer that fits into the gap grammatically. You have to choose the correct word that fits in terms of *meaning* as well as *grammar*.

Questions 13–20 ⏱ 13

Complete the summary below using words from the box.

According to the passage, the chocolate market is dominated by ... (13) ... brands. For this reason, confectioners spend large sums of money on ... (14) ... advertisements. In fact, in 1996, the amount spent totalled £94m.

However, it is also important for companies to allocate resources to developing ... (15) ... ideas. One example of this is the 'Flyte' bar, which was developed by Mars. Chocolate producers also try to increase sales by changing their customers' ... (16) ... habits. For example, if a product has an ... (17) ... image, it may be necessary to alter this.

A ... (18) ... switch in consumer behaviour can be achieved by introducing 'special edition' brands on to the market. These are successful because they offer ... (19) ... value. They also seem to increase the ... (20) ... sales of standard brands.

media	new	purchasing	outstanding	impulse	children's
limited	low-fat	serious	similar	well-known	novelty
outdated	overseas	eating	international	temporary	overall

Follow-up

21 How much of the passage does this summary cover?

22 Is the summary testing ideas or facts or both?

23 Can you identify the links between and within sentences?

Vocabulary builder

24 This text contains a lot of vocabulary that is typically used in the world of economics. Use the text and a dictionary to help you complete this table.

Noun	Verb	The person	Related phrases
a product **b** market /marketing **c** sales **d** growth **e** retail **f** brand **g** industry **h** stocks **i** launch	produce	producer/manufacturer	mass production

Reading

IELTS reading passages may focus on a research issue because academic study often involves reading research reports. Some IELTS questions focus on the arguments presented in this type of text, so it is useful to understand how the argument is developed.

FOLLOW THE LINE OF DEVELOPMENT

- Read the title and sub-heading below. What do you think the verb 'ape' means from your reading of the sub-heading? What points do you expect the article to cover?
- Think about how the writer might organise the article. What do you think will be included in the opening paragraph? What will form the body of the text. How will the text end?
- Now read the passage and complete the questions in the margin as you read.

Do apes ape?

Recent studies by two famous scientists show that chimpanzees and other apes can learn by imitation

What does paragraph A ask?

A The notion that the great apes – chimpanzees, gorillas, orang-utans and gibbons – can imitate one another might seem unsurprising to anyone who has watched these animals playing at the zoo. But in scientific circles, the question of whether apes really do 'ape', has become controversial.

What aspect of behaviour does paragraph B exemplify? Whose view is being considered?

B Consider a young chimpanzee watching his mother crack open a coula nut, as has been observed in the Taï Forest of West Africa. In most cases, the youth will eventually take up the practice himself. Was this because he imitated his mother? Sceptics think perhaps not. They argue that the mother's attention to the nuts encouraged the youngsters to focus on them as well. Once his attention had been drawn to the food, the young chimpanzee learned how to open the nut by trial and error, not by imitating his mother.

What is being discussed in paragraph C?

C Such a distinction has important implications for any discussion of chimpanzee cultures. Some scientists define a cultural trait as one that is passed down not by genetic inheritance but instead when the younger generation copies adult behaviour. If cracking open a coula nut is something that chimpanzees can simply figure out how to do on their own once they hold a hammer stone, then it can't be considered part of their culture. Furthermore, if these animals learn exclusively by trial and error, then chimpanzees must, in a sense, reinvent the wheel each time they tackle a new skill. No cumulative culture can ever develop.

What does paragraph D describe?

D The clearest way to establish how chimpanzees learn is through laboratory experiments. One of us (Whiten), in collaboration with Deborah M. Custance of Goldsmith's College, University of London, constructed artificial fruits to

52

serve as analogues of those the animals must deal with in the wild. In a typical experiment, one group of chimpanzees watched a complex technique for opening one of the fruits, while a second group observed a very different method; we then recorded the extent to which the chimpanzees had been influenced by the method they observed. We also conducted similar experiments with three-year-old children as subjects. Our results demonstrate that six-year-old chimpanzees show imitative behaviour that is markedly like that seen in the children, although the fidelity of their copying tends to be poorer.

What does paragraph E add to the previous paragraph?

E In a different kind of experiment, one of us (Boesch), along with some co-workers, gave chimpanzees in the Zurich Zoo in Switzerland hammers and nuts similar to those available in the wild. We then monitored the repertoire of behaviors displayed by the captive chimpanzees. As it turned out, the chimpanzees in the zoo exhibited a greater range of activities than the more limited and focused set of actions we had seen in the wild. We interpreted this to mean that a wild chimpanzee's cultural environment channelled the behavior of youngsters, steering them in the direction of the most useful skills. In the zoo, without the

benefit of existing traditions, the chimpanzees experimented with a host of less useful actions.

What does paragraph F suggest?

F Interestingly, some of the results from the experiments involving the artificial fruits converge with this idea. In one study, chimpanzees copied an entire sequence of actions they had witnessed, but did so only after several viewings and after trying some alternatives. In other words, they tended to imitate what they had observed others doing at the expense of their own trial-and-error discoveries.

What does paragraph G state?

G In our view, these findings taken together suggest that apes do ape and that this ability forms one strand in cultural transmission. Indeed, it is difficult to imagine how chimpanzees could develop certain geographic variations in activities such as ant-dipping and parasite-handling without copying established traditions. They must be imitating other members of their group.

What is the function of paragraph H?

H We should note, however, that – just as is the case with humans – certain cultural traits are no doubt passed on by a combination of imitation and simpler kinds of social learning, such as having one's attention drawn to useful tools. Either way, learning from elders is crucial to growing up as a competent wild chimpanzee.

Scientific American

LOCATING INFORMATION

Some IELTS questions focus on where certain information appears in the passage. Following the argument will help you answer the questions.

IELTS Reading

Questions 1–5 🕐 11

*The passage has eight paragraphs labelled **A–H**.*

Which paragraphs contain the following information?

1 a reference to a variety of ape activities that occur in the wild

2 the results of research on two different subject groups

3 an explanation of what opponents view as cultural behaviour

4 the research question being addressed in the passage

5 the results of research in two different environments

TEST TIP
Questions like these do not follow the order of information in the passage. It is helpful to underline the key words in each question before you scan the passage for answers.

RECOGNISE ARGUMENTS

TEST TIP

Although some statements may sound true, you also need to check that they are stated in the passage.

Once you have identified the line of development in a passage, you should be able to answer questions about particular arguments. Remember not to confuse an argument or point of view with a fact.

- Label the following sentences as A for argument or F for fact:

6 Young apes watch their parents as they feed.

7 Young chimpanzees learn how to open nuts by trial and error only.

8 A cultural trait must be gained through genetic inheritance.

9 Chimpanzees need to watch behaviour repeatedly before they can try copy to it.

10 Chimpanzee skills include ant-dipping and parasite handling.

MULTIPLE CHOICE – LIST SELECTION

TEST TIP

You can put your answers to these questions in any order on your answer sheet.

> **IELTS Reading**

Question 11 ⏱ 7

*Which **THREE** of the following arguments are stated by the writers of the passage?*

A Not everyone agrees that chimpanzees copy each other's behaviour.

B Chimpanzee behaviour depends on the type of tool that they use.

C Chimpanzee behaviour is best understood by observing them in their natural habitat.

D Children are better imitators than chimpanzees.

E Captive chimpanzees have a clearer idea of how to open nuts than those in the wild.

F Chimpanzees' observation of parent behaviour is vital to their development.

> **Vocabulary builder**

12 Scan the passage for the following words. Try to work out their meaning first, then look them up in the dictionary and decide on the correct meaning.

Word	Part of Speech	Meaning
notion	noun	belief or idea (collocates with 'vague')
controversial		
sceptics		
distinction		
implications		
exclusively		
collaboration		
imitative		
monitored		
converge		
crucial		

Reading

IELTS reading passages nearly always contain opinions, claims or views. These may be clearly stated or the reader may be able to infer them. Writers use a variety of ways to express their opinions and it is important to be able to recognise these while you are reading.

- First, read the text below and make notes about what the following people do or did.

  Dr Simon Cole   ....

  Francis Galton   ....

  Byron Mitchell   ....

  Robert Epstein   ....

Fingerprints

Fingerprints, the touchstone of forensic science, have never been subjected to proper scientific scrutiny

1 FOR most of the century since it made its courtroom debut, fingerprinting has enjoyed an impeccable reputation for identifying criminals. What jury would acquit a suspect if his prints matched those found at the scene of a crime? It was thus understandable that when a speaker at a recent meeting on Science and the Law held in San Diego by America's Justice Department hinted that the technique might not deserve its aura of infallibility, an FBI agent in the audience was later overheard calling him an unprintable name.

2 Understandable, but not, says the speaker, Simon Cole, justified. For he is one of a small group of people that has started looking at the technique which, above all others, gave forensic science its scientific status. And, surprisingly, he has found it is scientifically and statistically wanting.

3 This is not to say that the world's prisons are full of innocent victims of dodgy evidence. But the fact is, according to Dr Cole, who researched the subject at Cornell University, that fingerprinting has never been subjected to the scientific scrutiny required in a modern courtroom. And he thinks it should be.

4 Modern fingerprinting goes back to Francis Galton, a 19th-century British scientist who, ironically, helped to pioneer the use of statistics. In 1892 Galton looked at the pattern of whorls, arches and loops that make up fingerprints, and estimated that the chance of two prints matching at random was about one in 64 billion.

5   That estimate, however, has never been backed up by any data. Besides, Galton was not really comparing whole prints. Instead, he identified places where the ridges of which fingerprints are composed, either end or split. These are now known as 'points of similarity', or 'Galton details', and if two prints have enough points in common they are deemed to be identical.

6   Galton's estimate relied on using every available point (there are generally between 35 and 50). Current practice, which varies widely from one place to another, has been to declare a match if there are somewhere between eight and 16 points of similarity linking a print found at a crime scene and one taken from a suspect. Unfortunately, the validity of this process, and the number of points of similarity needed to make it statistically secure, have not been scientifically investigated. Nor has the alternative technique, recently introduced in England of relying on an examiner's overall impression of a match, without any attempt at quantification. That puts fingerprinting on shaky theoretical ground. And two other things make the situation worse in practice.

7   The first is that fingerprints found at crime scenes tend to be incomplete. What are being compared are thus not whole prints, but mere fragments. Nothing, not even Galton's original analysis, has anything to say about the likelihood of fragments of prints coinciding in different individuals.

8   The second difficulty is that most fingerprint evidence found at the scene of a crime is 'latent'. In other words it requires treatment with chemicals, or illumination with ultraviolet light, in order to make it visible enough to work with – and, even then, it is often indistinct. How valid it is to compare such 'filtered' evidence with the clean crisp prints obtained from suspects in controlled conditions is another unexplored question.

9   The upshot is that, at least by comparison with the techniques used to process DNA evidence (which are often, in tribute to the awe in which the older technique is held, referred to as 'DNA fingerprinting'), fingerprints look technically flawed. And lawyers – backed in America by a judgment made in 1993 that set standards for the admission of scientific evidence in court – are starting to notice.

The Economist

10   The turning point was the case of Byron Mitchell, who allegedly drove the getaway car in a robbery carried out in Pennsylvania in 1991. In 1998, Mr Mitchell appealed against his conviction. The case turned on two latent prints – one found on the getaway car's steering wheel and the other on its gear lever – that were said to link him to the crime.

11   The details of the case are tortuous; Mr Mitchell's conviction was upheld this year, but his lawyer Robert Epstein, another doubter of the value of fingerprints, is still trying to have it overturned. During the course of the trial, however the FBI did something that had never been done before. It carried out a rough and ready experiment to test the reliability of fingerprints.

12   It did this by sending the latent prints, plus inked prints of Mr Mitchell's fingers, to the laboratories of 53 state law enforcement agencies. Eight of the 35 agencies that responded were unable to find a match for one of the latent prints, and six failed to match the other – an average failure rate of 20%.

13   That is a shocking result. And confidence in the bureau's objective attitude to scientific evidence is not enhanced by its response to the first round of results. It slipped enlarged photographs of the latent prints and the prints from Mr Mitchell into transparent plastic sleeves, and marked red dots on the sleeves to suggest which of Mr Mitchell's prints matched the latent ones and where. When this 'modified' evidence was sent back to the errant laboratories, most of the examiners took the hint and agreed that the prints did actually match, after all.

14   This case, in Dr Cole's view, casts serious, and for the first time quantitative doubt on the reliability of fingerprints. More research would thus be welcome, and America's National Institute of Justice (an arm of the Department of Justice) is proposing to study the matter, and has made $500,000 available to do so. This is, in effect, an admission that fingerprinting as now practised may not actually be reliable. In the meantime, the use of a technique that may have an error rate as high as 20% raises a lot of legal questions. If these are not answered soon, many more cases that turned on a few smudges left behind by a careless criminal or an innocent bystander are going to be dragged before the appeal courts.

- What is your view of the use of fingerprints to convict criminals?
- What *two* new pieces of information have you learnt from this passage?

RECOGNISE THE WRITER'S VIEWS

A writer will use words, phrases and other stylistic techniques to express his or her views. For example, if the writer begins a sentence with 'It is unclear whether …' The reader should understand that the writer feels that something is *not certain or carries some doubt.*

- Find expressions in the text to match these definitions.

1 first appear / be shown (paragraph 1)

2 notice important things missing (paragraph 2)

3 have no firm foundation or basis (paragraph 6)

4 result or outcome (paragraph 9)

5 respect highly (paragraph 9)

6 critical moment (paragraph 10)

7 not very exact or serious (paragraph 11)

8 make appear less true (paragraph 14)

- Replace the words and phrases in italics in sentences 9–14 with one of the expressions. It may be necessary to change the sentence structure.

9 I *looked up* to my English Professor *so much* that I was stunned when I heard that he had lost his job.

10 The student had a rather *casual* attitude towards his studies and rarely managed to turn up at lectures.

11 The newspaper article *seriously questioned* the popular wisdom that vitamin C protects against the common cold.

12 The actors *first performed* in an old warehouse on the edge of town.

13 Jim's career *suddenly took off* when he got a job with a well-known IT company.

14 Pete had to accept that he *no longer enjoyed* his friends' company.

- Find examples of the following devices in the text.

15 a rhetorical question that suggests a certain viewpoint (paragraph 1)

16 an adverb that 'carries' an attitude or view (paragraph 2)

17 a structure that means 'I am not suggesting that…' (paragraph 3)

18 an expression used to give an opinion (paragraph 6)

YES, NO, NOT GIVEN

IELTS Reading

There is a similar question type to this that tests your understanding of factual information in the Academic Reading passage. In this case, you are asked to state whether the information is TRUE, FALSE or NOT GIVEN. The approach you should use in both question types, is the same. (See *Insight into IELTS* page 55.)

Pre-task questions

19 How should you approach the Yes, No, Not given task type?

20 What is the difference between 'No' and 'Not given' questions?

Questions 21–27 🕐 13

Do the following statements agree with the views of the writer in the reading passage? Write

> **YES**   *if the statement agrees with the writer*
>
> **NO**   *if the statement contradicts the writer*
>
> **NOT GIVEN**   *if it is impossible to say what the writer thinks about this*

21 If a suspect's fingerprints match those found at the scene of a crime, a jury is expected to find that person guilty.

22 It is surprising that criminal experts were reluctant to accept any criticism of fingerprinting.

23 Simon Cole's initial findings were to be expected.

24 Many of today's prisoners are actually innocent people who have been wrongly convicted.

25 There are surprising gaps in Galton's research on fingerprinting.

26 Fingerprints cannot successfully be taken on the ground.

27 Further investigation is needed into the way fingerprints are compared.

Vocabulary builder

Some words are used together so often in English that using other words with a similar meaning sounds wrong. For example, we tend to say that someone has a *strong* argument against something rather than a *heavy* argument. We say that strong collocates with argument.

- Look at the list of nouns 28–36. Choose a verb from the box below that collocates with each one. More than one answer may be possible.

28 a reputation

29 confidence

30 an experiment

31 status

32 questions

33 a robbery

34 scrutiny

35 argument

36 a conviction

subject (to)		back up (by/with)		enjoy	enhance
give	raise	increase		uphold	carry out

- Complete the gaps in the following sentences by using an appropriate verb in the correct tense/voice. More than one answer may be possible.

37 After the lecture some of the students .... some interesting questions about the reliability of the data and the experiments that had ....

38 Many academics carry out research in order to .... their good reputation in the field and .... their status within the university.

39 At the appeal of his first trial the defendant finally admitted that he had .... the robbery and his conviction was therefore ....

40 The passengers were .... considerable scrutiny at the airport which did little to .... their confidence in the airline.

41 The politician was unable to .... any of his arguments and soon found that he could no longer .... the reputation he once had.

Reading

SHORT ANSWER QUESTIONS

IELTS Reading

Short answer questions require a brief response in your own words but you will never be asked to write more than three words.

Questions 1–10 🕐 10

*Look at the texts below. Using **NO MORE THAN THREE WORDS**, answer questions 1–10.*

Picasso Museum

Chateau Grimaldi Antibes France

The Picasso Museum of Antibes is housed in a beautiful old villa built on ground that was once occupied by the ancient Greeks and later by the Romans. Picasso himself lived in the house and painted there in 1946.

Guided tours can be organised on request. There are several programs for children (ages 4–11) and workshop visits for school groups on Wednesdays and holidays.

June 1 – Sept 30   10am–6pm
Oct1 – May 31   10am–noon and 2–6pm
Closed Mondays and holidays

NATIONAL MARITIME MUSEUM

WHAT'S ON today?
- ◆ Tall Ships on the harbour
- ◆ Visit the "Vampire" destroyer
- ◆ 'Macquarie Lighthouse' – short film in theatrette

CAFÉ
Refreshments with views of the harbour.

MUSEUM SHOP
Crammed with books and unusual souvenirs.

VOLUNTEERS
Opportunities exist for interested people to donate their time by becoming tour guides at the museum. Enquire at the Volunteers' desk.

PHOTOGRAPHY
Use of flash not permitted inside the Museum.

HOURS
10am–5.00pm Daily Except Christmas Day

1 Where is the Picasso Museum? *In a old villa France*

2 Who once lived there? *Picasso*

3 When are children most welcome? *Wed/ holiday*

4 Which months is it open all day? *Jne-Sep*

5 How do you get a guided tour? *request for it*

6 How many events are on today? *3*

7 What can you see from the café? *harbour view*

8 How much are the tour guides paid? *nothing*

9 What should you not do here? *a flash camera*

10 When is the museum closed to the public? *Xmas day*

TRUE, FALSE, NOT GIVEN

In this type of task, you will read a text followed by some statements.
If the statements agree with the information in the original, write 'True'.
If the statements give the opposite meaning to the information in the original, write 'False'.
If there was no mention of this information in the original, write 'Not Given'.

IELTS Reading (GT)

- Read the text and answer questions 11–16.
- Underline the words in the text which gave you the answer.
- If the information is not given in the text, is there anything which might lead you to give the wrong answer?

Fremantle Prison
Western Australia's Premier Cultural Hertitage Site

Fremantle Prison is a 14-acre walled enclosure built in 1850 from limestone, quarried on the site. The complex includes the main block, the old bake house, the workshop and hospital. Today the buildings stand empty and are open to the public.

Visiting Times
Monday to Sunday 10am–5pm (7 days a week)
Friday 7.30pm Candlelight tours (bookings only)
Closed Christmas Day and Good Friday

Tours
School Tours available

Amenities
Café Souvenirs Photographer

Well worth a visit!

Questions 11–16 ⊘8

Read the advertisement above and look at the statements below (Questions 11–16).

Write

TRUE	*if the statement agrees with the information in the passage*
FALSE	*if the statement contradicts the information in the passage*
NOT GIVEN	*if there is no information about this in the passage*

11 The stone comes from the ground on which the prison was built.   True

12 Fremantle prison functions as a working prison today.   False!

13 The prison is open every day of the year.   False

14 Hundreds of visitors come to the prison every year.   Not given

15 You need to book ahead for the night visit.   True

16 You cannot take photographs within the buildings.

Questions 17–22 ⏱ 8

Read the leaflet below and look at the statements below (Questions 17–22).

Write

TRUE   *if the statement agrees with the information in the passage*
FALSE   *if the statement contradicts the information in the passage*
NOT GIVEN   *if there is no information about this in the passage*

17 You are asked to take care of the fragile Australian environment.
18 You can always change money at the hotels.
19 You run the greatest risk of sunburn at the beach.
20 You can only swim if there are lifeguards on the beach.
21 Many native animals are killed on the roads at night.
22 It is illegal to ride a bicycle without wearing a helmet.

Welcome to Australia!
Essential Information for Travellers

The Great Outdoors

Australia is the world's oldest continent and indigenous Australians have one of the world's oldest cultures.

In Australia you will see unique plants and animals and some of the most beautiful scenery in the world. Many parks have information centres offering advice on where to go, what to see and how to see it – for both your personal safety and to protect our sensitive, natural environment.

Banks and money matters

Banks are generally open between 9.30 and 4.00pm on Monday to Thursday and 9.30 and 5.00pm on Friday.

Foreign currency or traveller's cheques can be changed at all banks and some of the larger hotels. There are currency exchange facilities at all international airports.

The Sun

Take care! Our sunlight is very strong and you can get sunburnt.

For best sun protection, it is advisable to wear:
* broad brimmed hat
* shirt with collar and sleeves
* sun screen with high protection factor

Swimming

We have so many beautiful places to swim – beaches, lakes, rivers and creeks.
* Many of our waters are safe for swimming, but if you have any doubts, ask before entering the water.
* Most of our popular ocean beaches have patrols with lifesaving service. Red and yellow flags mark the area that you are advised to swim within.
* If there are no flags and no lifeguards on the beach, talk to local people about the best areas to swim.

Staying safe on the roads

* Australians drive on the LEFT hand side of the road.
* For safety, everyone in the car, including children, must wear a seatbelt.
* Motor cyclists and bicyclists are required to wear a helmet.
* Watch out for native animals crossing the roads, especially at night. Road signs are erected in places where animals are commonly seen.

Have a wonderful time in Australia!

Reading

Section 2 of the General Training module uses similar task types to Section 1. The texts are longer but the focus is still on your ability to understand factual information.

PARAGRAPH HEADINGS

This type of question tests your global reading skills. On page 64 of *Insight into IELTS* you will find advice on how to approach this type of task.

- Read through the passage to get a general idea of the topic.
- Then read the headings below and match them to the paragraphs.
- There will always be one or two more headings than you need.

IELTS Reading (GT)

Questions 1–6 ⏱ 10

The reading passage has six paragraphs A–F.

From the list of headings below choose the most suitable heading for each paragraph.

List of Headings
i   Cultural activities
ii   Exchange programs
iii   Formal means of assessment
iv   Getting around the campus
v   Financial assistance
vi   Special consideration
vii   University by-laws
viii   Identification
ix   Study skills workshops
x   Essay writing

Example	Answer
Paragraph A	**x** / o

1 Paragraph B   iii

2 Paragraph C   vi

3 Paragraph D   ii

4 Paragraph E   v

5 Paragraph F   ~~x~~ viii

6 Paragraph G   i

UNIVERSITY SERVICES
Essential information for students

A For many courses in the University, the majority of your marks will be based on your written work. It is essential that you develop your skills as a writer for the different disciplines in which you study. Most departments offer advice and guidelines on how to present your written assignments but you should be aware that the requirements may vary from one department to another.

B There are two formal examination periods each year; first semester period beginning in June and the second semester period beginning in November. Additionally, individual departments may examine at other times and by various methods such as 'take-home' exams, assignments, orally, practical work and so on.

C If you feel your performance in an examination has been adversely affected by illness or misadventure, you should talk to the course Co-ordinator in your department and complete an appropriate form. Each case is considered on its own merits.

D The University has arrangements with universities throughout the United States, Canada, Europe and Asia. The schemes are open to undergraduate and postgraduate students and allow you to complete a semester or a year of your degree overseas. The results you gain are credited towards your degree at this university. This offers an exciting and challenging way of broadening your horizons and enriching your academic experience in a different environment and culture.

E Youth Allowance may be available to full-time students. Reimbursement of travel costs may also be available in some cases. Postgraduate research funds are offered for full-time study towards Masters by Research or PhD degrees. These are competitive and the closing date for applications is 31 October in the year prior to the one for which the funds are sought.

F Your student card, obtained on completion of enrolment, is proof that you are enrolled. Please take special care of it and carry it with you when you're at the university. You may be asked to show it to staff at any time. This card is also your discount card and access card for the Students' Union as well as allowing you access to the library.

G The Union provides opportunities for a wide range of activities, from the production of films and plays, to concerts and magazines, and even art and photo exhibitions. If you have a creative idea in mind, pick up a form from ACCESS on Level 3, Wandsworth Building.

Vocabulary builder

- Read the text again and find words which have the same meaning as the following definitions. These are all words which you are likely to meet at a college or university.

	Word used in text
a subject you can study at university	7 .... ~~topic~~ *disciplines*
a statement which gives rules and regulations about something	8 .... *guideline*
a piece of work, normally written, set by your teacher, often with a deadline	9 .... *assignment*
a division of the academic year	10 .... *semester*
one of the sections of a school, college or university	11 .... *department*
a person who organises a course	12 .... ~~female~~ *coordinator*
a qualification you study for at a university	13 .... *degree*
money which is given back to you *research*	14 .... *reimbursement*
original work done by a student as part of his or her studies ✗	15 .... ~~performance~~
to register at a university for a course ✗	16 .... *enrolment* *to enrol*
a display of artwork	17 .... *exhibition*

- Using words from the vocabulary builder list, complete this passage which offers advice to new students. Use one word only for each space.

Advice for new students *enrol*

When you first arrive at a college or university, you will need to … **(18)** … in the subjects that you have chosen to study.

This process can take the best part of a day, so be prepared to wait around!

For each course there is a … **(19)** … *coordinator*, who is responsible for organising the program and you should make sure that you introduce yourself to him or her early in the … **(20)** … *semester*. In that way, if you need to make any changes to your program, you will know who to speak to.

The form of assessment for each course varies from department to … **(21)** … *department* but most will use a combination of examinations and … **(22)** … *a.* . If you are studying for a higher … **(23)** … *degree* a lot of your work may involve personal … **(24)** … *research* Most universities have strict … **(25)** … *guideline* governing the amount of time allowed to complete such a program.

- Now write five sentences using at least two of the words in each sentence, to show you understand how they function.

MATCHING

Matching is another common type of IELTS question designed to test your ability to skim and scan.

IELTS Reading (GT)

Questions 26–34 13

*Look at the following statements about books (Questions 26–34) and the information about some new books **A–F** on a bookshop website.*

Match each statement to the correct book.

TEST TIP

There may be more than one statement about each of the books.

This book:

26 will help you keep fit and feel good.   F

27 is for the urban history student.   D

28 is for the reader with an interest in maritime history. B

29 is a light-hearted look at successful money management. C

30 is by a well published author.   E

31 explores human motivation and character.   A

32 is the author's first publication.   A

33 provides practical advice on how to present yourself.   E

34 is recommended as a present.   F

? Student help desk   **Shopping basket**   **About us**   **Web books e-catalogue**

A Around the World in 80 weeks
By David Franklin

Franklin's debut book is a story of courage and personal achievement. Based on his experiences sailing single-handed around the world, a voyage that took him over a year and a half to complete, it offers the reader an insight into what compels some individuals to set sail alone, in search of excitement and themselves. An extraordinary account from a new author with a great future ahead.

B A long way from home
By Anita Bloom

This is the tail of the Sydney Cove, a three masted ship which departed Calcutta on 10 November 1796 for Australia. Gale force winds and heavy seas soon caused huge damage forcing the Captain to beach the waterlogged Sydney Cove on an Island – just off Tasmania. Bloom's attention to historical detail makes this a fascinating story and one you won't want to put down.

C On a Shoe String
By Claire Ribeiro

This is a must for every young person trying to make ends meet. Shoe String is packed with helpful hints and practical ideas on how to make your budget stretch while still managing to enjoy life. Ribeiro's keen sense of humour shines through on every page.

D Post post modernity – where to next?
By Karl Kapstad

Buildings, art, fashion, design. Kapstad takes a long look at how form has changed over the last 40 years and comes up with some fascinating predictions for the future.

E Dressed for Life
By Mavis E. Marquick

Mavis Marquick has been writing about fashion for years but she's still got something new to say to us all. Marquick takes the view that your clothes are what people notice first about you and remember last! So why make a bad impression. But you don't need to spend a fortune to look good – you just need an eye for colour and occasion. Buy the book to benefit from Mavis' years of experience in the cut and thrust world of fashion!

F You are what you eat.
By Dr. Susan Low

A young person's guide to healthy living and eating.
This little book is stuffed full of recipes, exercises and great ideas for making the most of your larder, while keeping your body in good shape. Students note the price –makes a great gift.

Writing

UNIT 1 Describing facts and figures Academic Task 1

Before you begin a description of a graph or chart, you need to have an accurate understanding of its content.

GET THE FACTS RIGHT!

World's top languages
Millions of speakers (as first or second language)

Chinese	1,123
English	470
Hindi	418
Spanish	372
Russian	288
Bengali	235
Arabic	235
Portuguese	182
Japanese	125
French	124
German	121

> **TEST TIP**
> When you do Task 1, it is important to look carefully at the diagram, graph or chart. It is easy to misinterpret the information and if you provide factually incorrect information in your answer, you will lose marks.

1 What is wrong with this statement?

Chinese is the world's most widely-spoken language, with 1,123 speakers.

2 What *two* things are wrong with this statement?

Only 121 people speak German, which is the world's least-spoken language.

3 Complete this description with information from the chart and words from the box. You may use the words more than once.

widely	higher	least	Russian	second	smallest	most	relatively

The chart shows the world's top ten languages. These include the main European and Indian languages as well as ...... **a** ...... and Arabic. According to the graph, Chinese is the ...... **b** ...... widely used language in the world with ...... **c** ...... speakers. English is the ...... **d** ...... most popular language with a total of ...... **e** ...... speakers. Hindi is also very ...... **f** ...... spoken and in fourth place we find Spanish, which is the ...... **g** ...... most popular European language, closely followed by Russian, Bengali and Arabic. The number of Japanese speakers currently stands at ...... **h** ...... which, we can see, is slightly ...... **i** ...... than the 124 million French speakers. The ...... **j** ...... widely spoken language mentioned in the chart is German which has the ...... **k** ...... small number of 121 million speakers.

BE PRECISE

Although you may read the charts or graphs correctly, you could still lose marks if you do not state the facts *clearly* and *precisely*.

• Read the title of this table and the list of subjects. Can you say in your own words what information the chart contains?

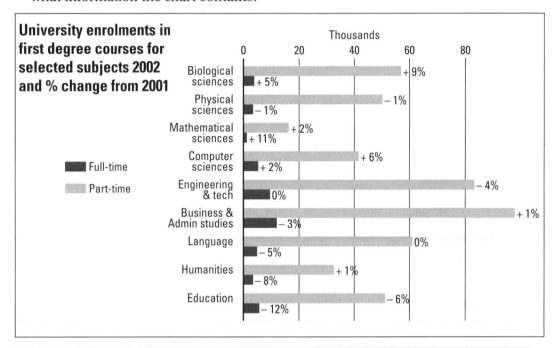

University enrolments in first degree courses for selected subjects 2002 and % change from 2001

Thousands

Full-time
Part-time

Biological sciences + 9% / + 5%
Physical sciences − 1% / − 1%
Mathematical sciences + 2% / + 11%
Computer sciences + 6% / + 2%
Engineering & tech − 4% / 0%
Business & Admin studies + 1% / − 3%
Language 0% / − 5%
Humanities + 1% / − 8%
Education − 6% / − 12%

'Being precise' often means writing longer sentences. It also involves thinking about the vocabulary and phrases that you will use *before* you begin writing your answer.

4 Add more words to this table which would help you describe the chart on enrolments.

Nouns	Adjectives	Verbs	Adverbs	Phrases
enrolment	high(er)	enrol	slightly	just under

- Look at the chart carefully, then make the following sentences more accurate and/or precise, adding more detail where you feel necessary.

5 Enrolments went down for a lot of subjects.

Full- and part-time enrolments remained the same or went down in most subjects, apart from biological, mathematical and computer sciences courses where student numbers increased.

6 Twenty thousand students enrolled in Mathematical sciences in the year 2001.

7 Sixty full-time students enrolled in Language courses in the year 2002.

8 The number of students who enrolled in Physical sciences went up by one per cent.

9 In 2002, twelve part-time students dropped out of Education courses.

10 In 2001, there were no part-time students on Engineering courses.

11 There was a six per cent increase in enrolments on Computer sciences courses in 2002.

DESCRIBE THE DATA – DO NOT EXPLAIN IT

You may feel that you can *explain* some of the data. However, you are not expected to do this. In fact, any information that you provide that is not supplied in the diagram will be ignored by the examiner and you may lose marks for irrelevance.

- The following table and pie chart provide information on the ages of people who, in an interview on television viewing habits, said they watched a well-known soap opera.

12 Why are both the table and the pie chart useful?

13 What words, phrases or expressions might help you describe this data precisely?

Age-group	No.
Below 20	225
21–25	758
26–30	258
31–35	150
36–40	76
40+	43
Total	**1510**

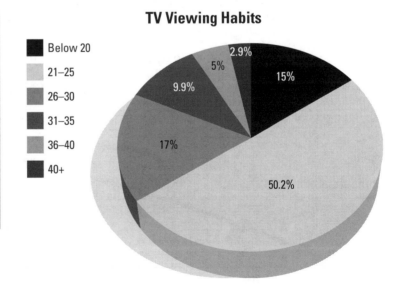

TV Viewing Habits

Below 20
21–25
26–30
31–35
36–40
40+

2.9%
5%
15%
9.9%
17%
50.2%

14 Read the sample paragraph below and identify the parts which are irrelevant to the description of the table and pie chart.

15 Correct the sample answer, following the notes given, and re-write the irrelevant sections.

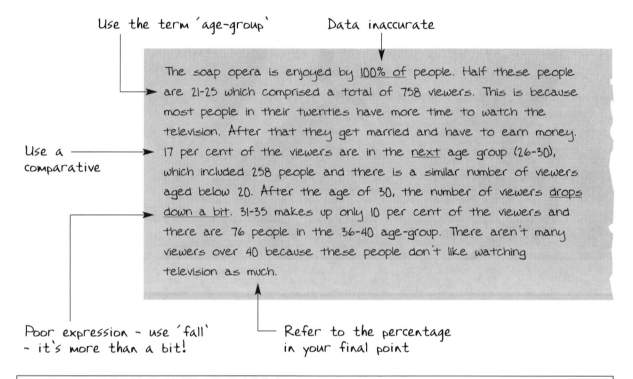

Use the term 'age-group'

Data inaccurate

Use a comparative

Poor expression – use 'fall' – it's more than a bit!

Refer to the percentage in your final point

The soap opera is enjoyed by 100% of people. Half these people are 21-25 which comprised a total of 758 viewers. This is because most people in their twenties have more time to watch the television. After that they get married and have to earn money. 17 per cent of the viewers are in the next age group (26-30), which included 258 people and there is a similar number of viewers aged below 20. After the age of 30, the number of viewers drops down a bit. 31-35 makes up only 10 per cent of the viewers and there are 76 people in the 36-40 age-group. There aren't many viewers over 40 because these people don't like watching television as much.

APPROACHING THE TASK – 1

When you write a description of a graph or chart you need to begin by referring to the 'subject' or 'topic', e.g.
This graph shows the number of cars on the road every day.
The information in this chart relates to worldwide sales of soft drinks.

16 Write a sentence to describe chart a, and include the word 'compare'.

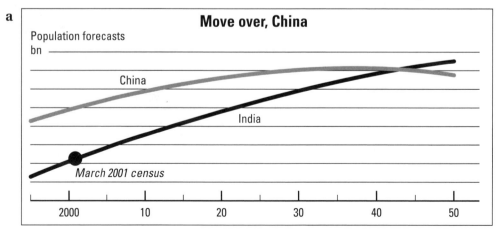

a

Move over, China

17 What is the topic of chart b? Write a sentence that begins: 'The graph shows…'

18 What is the topic of chart c? Write a sentence to describe chart c including the words 'selected countries'.

b

c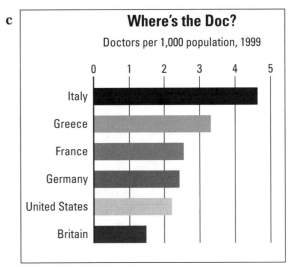

19 Use the sets of words to write sentences describing this pie chart.

An Athlete's Dietary Requirements

athlete's diet / consist / large / carbohydrate

60% / daily diet / carbohydrates

second / important / food group / fat / account / 25% / diet

smallest / protein

proportion / food group / 15% / total

Writing

Line graphs and bar charts often show trends. Though these trends may have variations within them, it is important to look, for an 'overall trend' first.

INCREASING OR DECREASING TRENDS

- Look at this bar chart. The information it presents shows a consistent overall trend.

a
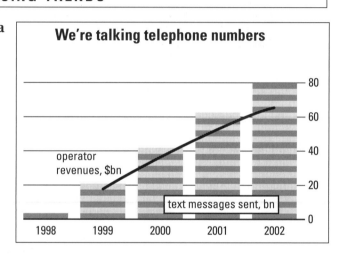

▶ First ask yourself these questions:

What is the chart about?

What does the horizontal axis show?

What does the vertical axis show?

What overall trend(s) does the graph show?

- Look at the chart carefully, then complete these two descriptions of the overall trend.

1 Between .... and .... the global number of text messages sent rose steadily.

2 There was .... in the global number of text messages sent ....

- Refer to page 69 of *Insight into IELTS* for more language that can be used to describe trends.

- Now complete this sentence which describes the overall trend and includes more figures.

3 The number of text messages sent worldwide rose from .... in .... to .... in ....

STABILITY

Some patterns or trends in graphs do not change over time, or change so little that they are said to be 'stable'.

- Look at the examples of 'stability' shown in graphs b and c.

b **Hoop dreams**

Basketball attendance per regular season home game, '000

NBA average

Dallas Mavericks average

1995-97 1997-98 1998-99 1999-2000 2000-01

NBA = National Basketball Association

c **Jay's Sports Club Membership (previous year)**

Fully-paid

J F M A M J J A S O N D

4   Write two sentences which describe the overall trends shown in graph b.

5   Write two or more sentences to form a short paragraph which describes graph c.

FLUCTUATION

When a graph rises or falls irregularly it is said to fluctuate. Sometimes there is still an overall trend, upwards, downwards or stable, but with lots of small irregular changes.

6   Re-write this sentence adding an adjective or adjectival phrase commonly used with the noun 'fluctuation'. There may be several possibilities.

   Over the decades there has been fluctuation in the number of people who vote in elections in the UK.

7   Look at this graph. In order to avoid repetition in your writing, what is another way of saying 'demand for electricity'?

8   Write a one-sentence description of the graph that provides an overall picture of the trend.

d **Demand for electricity during a televised World Cup football match**

Units

29,000

28,000

27,000

26,000

Start of match   Half time   Full time   End of extra time

19:00 hrs   20:00 hrs   21:00 hrs   22:00 hrs   23:00 hrs

9 Write five more sentences about graph d, using the prompts below:

At the start ....

There is a .... during the first .... but then

Demand falls again .... lowest point

In the last forty minutes ....

However, at the beginning .... plateau .... resume normal

---

APPROACHING THE TASK – 2

> After you have introduced a graph or chart by explaining what the topic is and what the graph generally shows, you then need to provide a more detailed description of the graph. This can often begin with a statement about the overall trend.

- Select one of the graphs in Unit 1 or 2 and write an opening paragraph that could come before your detailed description of it.

- Look at the graph and the sample description of it below.

10 What is wrong with the writer's approach to this task? Write the part that is missing.

A degree of progress

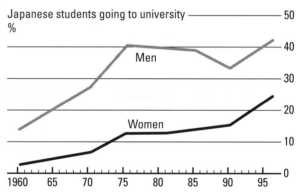

Japanese students going to university %

11 Now complete the gaps in the answer by using an appropriate word to describe the patterns shown.

Sample answer

The ... **a** ... in the number of women going to university has been fairly ... **b** ... although in the last ten years figures have ... **c** ... more ... **d** ... Currently, it is estimated that 25 per cent of Japanese women receive a university education. This is still a .... **e** ... percentage than the male figure.

The male pattern shows more ... **f** ... particularly between 1970 and 1975, when figures ... **g** ... by 15 per cent to a ... **h** ... of 40 per cent. This represents the greatest period of increase and it was followed by a ... **i** ... in numbers between 1975 and 1980. Overall, however, the two ... **j** ... are similar and the recent rate of increase for men ... **k** ... that of women, leading to a present-day figure of just over 40 per cent.

Writing

In addition to describing the topic of the graph/chart/diagrams and any *overall* trends or features, you should highlight any significant details or data. To do this, you will need to select and group your points in an organised way.

DESCRIBE SIGNIFICANT DETAILS

- Look at these two graphs and answer questions 1–5 about the first graph.

1 What is another useful term for 'Fertility' that you could use in your answer?
2 What do the figures on the vertical axis of this graph represent?
3 Which trend in this graph do you think is most significant?
4 Which of the statistics do you find most surprising?
5 How do you know that you will need to use a variety of tenses?

The graphs below give information on the world population and the average number of children per family in developed and developing countries.

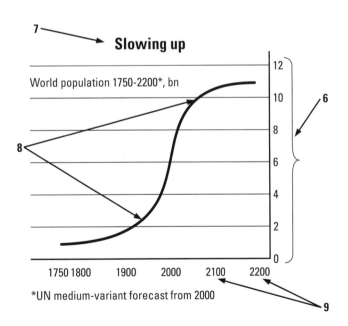

- Now look at the second graph. Arrows 6–9 point to important features of this graph. State briefly what these features are.

THINK ABOUT HOW YOU WILL ORGANISE YOUR ANSWER

When you write your description, you should start by outlining the topic and overall trends. If you have more than one graph or chart, you also need to decide which one to describe first. Then, you need to select certain details on the graphs to highlight. You may be able to end by making a concluding point *but this must be based on the information in the task.*

10 Which of the graphs above would you choose to describe first?

11 How would you relate the two graphs?

12 Which feature of the first graph would you highlight first?

13 How might you end your answer?

As stated in Unit 2, it is helpful to divide your answer into paragraphs. The information that you put in each paragraph will depend on the task and the features that you decide to highlight.

14 Read the sample answer to the task on page 75 and complete the summary of each paragraph in the right-hand column.

The graphs give information about global birth rates and population size. They predict that the global population growth rate will begin to decrease towards the middle of this century and will eventually stabilise at approximately 11 billion.

Since the mid 20th century, the world's population has risen dramatically, from 2 billion to 7 billion. However, we should soon begin to see a fall in the population growth rate that will become more marked as we move into the 22nd century.

These changes are largely due to falling birth rates in developing countries. In 1950, the average number of children per family in developing countries was 6.2. Between 1950 and the present day, this figure has fallen significantly to 3.3 and it is predicted to decrease further to 2.1 children per family in 2050.

Birth rates have also fallen in developed countries over the past 50 years, from 2.8 children per family to 1.6. Projected figures for 2050 show a slight increase in the birth rate in these areas and predict, interestingly, the same birth rate for both developing and developed countries.

a   Gives...

b   Describes...

c   Links...

d   Describes...

e   Describes...

- Underline all the verbs in the answer. Why have different tenses been used?

- Collect some graphs and charts and practise talking about them with your study partner or friend. Look at each one for *two minutes* then name the topic; describe what the graph/chart is about; describe any overall trends; describe any significant features; and discuss how you would organise a description of the information.

THINK ABOUT PARAGRAPH STRUCTURE AND LINKS

- Look at the bar chart below and add suitable words which could be used in a description of it.

spend time	sedentary	unlike	pursuits
most popular	unsurprising		

15 Are there any significant details in the chart?

16 In which order do you think the information should be presented in a description?

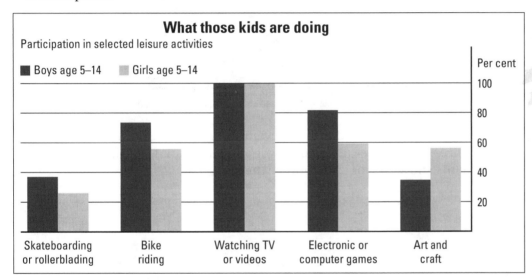

What those kids are doing

Participation in selected leisure activities

■ Boys age 5–14   ■ Girls age 5–14

Per cent

Skateboarding or rollerblading | Bike riding | Watching TV or videos | Electronic or computer games | Art and craft

TEST TIP

Describing graphs and charts often involves making comparisons. Comparative structures and phrases form useful links between points.

17 Look at the sample answer below and underline all the comparative structures and phrases.

The graph shows the preferred leisure activities of Australian children aged 5–14. As might be expected, it is clear from the data that sedentary pursuits are far more popular nowadays than active ones.

Of the 10,000 children that were interviewed, all the boys and girls stated that they enjoyed watching TV or videos in their spare time. In addition, the second most popular activity, attracting 80% of boys and 60% of girls, was playing electronic or computer games. While girls rated activities such as art and craft highly – just under 60% stated that they enjoyed these in their spare time – only 35% of boys opted for creative pastimes. Bike riding, on the other hand, was almost as popular as electronic games amongst boys and, perhaps surprisingly, almost 60% of girls said that they enjoyed this too. Skateboarding was relatively less popular amongst both boys and girls, although it still attracted 35% of boys and 25% of girls.

- Refer to page 74 of *Insight into IELTS* for more language that can be used to make comparisons.

18 Write a full description of the chart on student enrolments on page 68.

- The graph below gives information on the importation of products in Mexico. Before you read the sample answer below, think about a collective term that could be used for these products.

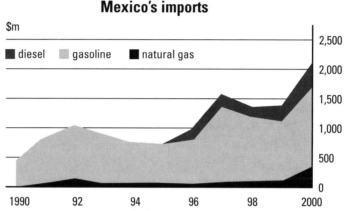

Mexico's imports

TEST TIP

The vertical axis should not be read by adding up each shaded area. The amount of gasoline that is imported is far greater than the other two.

19 The sample answer includes the relevant information, but the points could be better linked and the student could get a higher mark for it. Read the teacher's comments and see if you can improve the answer.

a What is the graph about? Needs an introductory sentence. Re-structure this paragraph and combine the three sentences.

b Combine this sentence with the next two.

c Add a final sentence to this paragraph which compares expenditure on gasoline with the other products.

d Less than what? How much less? Relate to previous paragraph.

e Combine these two sentences and re-phrase.

Sample answer

There has been a big increase in imports. Mexico's total imports of energy-based products reached the 2 billion-dollar mark in the year 2,000. In 1990, the figure was low at $500m.

The graph gives figures for diesel, gasoline and natural gas. Imports of gasoline have grown. There has been some fluctuation. In 2,000 the expenditure had increased to approximately $1,250m.

Expenditure on diesel and gasoline is less. About $1m was spent on importing each in 1990. More diesel has been imported since 1995. Five years later about $400m was spent on this product. Natural gas is similar. The growth in expenditure has a slightly different pattern.

Before you attempt to write your description for task 1, make sure you know how to *read* the data. Remember that it is important to be *accurate, precise* and *relevant*. Then think about how you will structure your answer and the vocabulary you will use.

IELTS Writing (Academic)	Task 1

Pre-task questions

20 What is meant by £/w and £/year?

21 What is meant by the term '2 bed' ?

22 What is another word for 'area' in this context?

23 How can you describe a house with three bedrooms using a compound adjective?

24 What is the purpose in this table of showing both the rental prices and the salaries data together?

🕐 20 | *The table below provides information on rental charges and salaries in three areas of London.*

Write a report for a university lecturer describing the information shown below.

Area	Weekly rents per property (£/w)			Salaries needed (£/year)		
	1 bed	2 bed	3 bed	1 bed	2 bed	3 bed
Notting Hill	375	485	738	98,500	127,500	194,000
Regent's Park	325	450	650	85,500	118,000	170,500
Fulham	215	390	600	56,500	102,500	157,500

You should write at least 150 words.

Writing

Sometimes the IELTS writing task is a picture or diagram rather than a graph or chart. However, you are still expected to describe only what you see and to organise the information in a logical way.

STUDY THE DIAGRAM CAREFULLY

- Look at the following *mini-task* about acid rain.

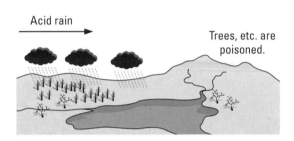

▶ First ask yourself:

What is the diagram about/what does it show?

What type of diagram is it?

- In answering these questions, you may need to ask yourself other questions about details on the diagram, such as:

1 What do the arrows show?

2 What is a collective term for trees and plants?

3 What buildings are shown?

- Before you begin writing your description, you will also need to decide *how* to write it.

4 What tense will you use? Why?

5 How will you organise the description?

- Before you go on, try writing a description of the diagram in a few sentences.

TEST TIP

Diagrams often include a lot of words. Although you can use some of these words, it is important that you write your own sentences. Anything copied directly from the diagram will be ignored by the examiner.

USE APPROPRIATE LINKERS

- Now read this description.

> The diagram shows how acid rain is formed. Initially, heavy industry emits pollutants such as sulphur and nitrogen into the atmosphere. These pollutants are then carried by the wind and deposited far away as acid rain. Eventually this kills vegetation and poisons water resources.

TEST TIP
You need to indicate the steps or stages in a process by using relevant linkers.

6 Which linkers show the steps in the process?

ORGANISE THE INFORMATION LOGICALLY

- Here is another diagram of a process.

> This is a more detailed diagram so in addition to asking yourself the questions on page 80, you also need to decide how to organise the information. As with graphs/charts, it is helpful to divide your answer into paragraphs.

- Study the diagram for 2–3 minutes and then answer the following questions.
 7 What is the topic of the diagram?
 8 What vocabulary will be useful for your answer?
 9 What information from the diagram could you include in a general first paragraph about the topic or subject matter?
10 What is a logical starting point for a description of the process (i.e. the second paragraph)?
11 Is it possible to split the description into two parts? If so, what could you describe in the third and final paragraph?

TEST TIP
Even if you know a lot about the subject matter, remember that you should only include information that you see in the diagram.

• Now read this sample description of the diagram on page 81.

> It is believed that the chain began to form nearly 80 million years ago. Each island started to evolve after an eruption on the sea floor. First, a 'hot spot' developed on the ocean bed, which let out a plume of material called magma. This magma may originate as deep as 283km below the ocean bed. Next, further eruptions took place, which built up the volcano. Eventually it emerged above the surface of the ocean.
>
> The Hawaiian island chain is a long chain in the ocean. It is very famous and people often like to visit this area for their holidays. It is formed of volcanoes, and the active ones are at the south-east tip of the archipelago, where Hawaii itself is located.
>
> Since that time, the spume of magma has remained static as the Pacific tectonic plate moves in a north-west direction across it at a speed of 7-9m per year. The hot spot makes new volcanoes all the time.

TEST TIP

Any of these errors will cause you to lose marks.

• Find the following:

12 one error in organisation.

13 two areas of inaccuracy.

14 two sentences that are imprecise.

15 one example of irrelevance.

16 Rewrite the answer, correcting all the errors that have been made.

• When you have finished, underline all the linkers that indicate the steps in the process.

• Complete the following which summarises the organisation of the answer:

TEST TIP

You may write only two paragraphs or as many as four paragraphs. This will depend on how you can best organise the information.

1st paragraph ....

2nd paragraph ....

3rd paragraph ....

IELTS Writing (Academic)	Task 1

⏱ 20

The diagrams below give information about the Eiffel Tower in Paris and an outline project to extend it underground.

Write a report for a university lecturer describing the information shown.

You should write at least 150 words.

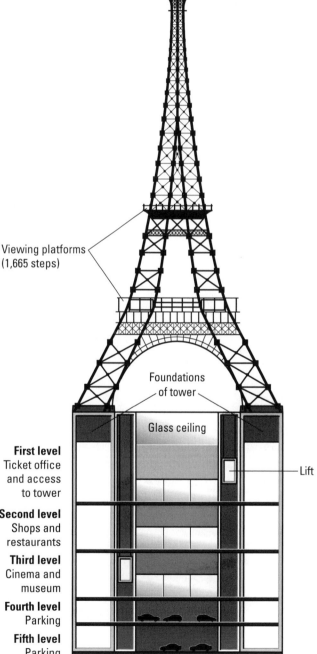

EIFFEL TOWER

Height: 324m

Weight of metal structure: 10,100 tonnes

First platform: 57m

Second platform: 115m

Writing

UNIT 5 General Training, Task 1

STUDY THE TASK CAREFULLY

In order to help you understand the purpose of your letter, General Training Writing Task 1 is presented using bullet points. The bullet points are really a list of content points and you should make sure that you cover them all, otherwise you will lose marks.

- Read this example of a GT Writing task.

  You recently took a part-time job working for a local company. After a few weeks, you realised there were some problems with the job.

  Write a letter to the manager of the company. In your letter
  - *explain why you took the job*
  - *describe the problems that you experienced*
  - *suggest what could be done about them*

1 Complete these notes about what you will need to include in the letter.

Decide on a type of .... and ....

Give reasons for ....

Give details of ....

Offer .... to problems

- Here are some possible jobs. Can you identify them?

84

- Complete the table below for jobs a–c. Try to think of two main points for each column.

- Then think of two more possible jobs, d and e, and complete the table.

Job	Why I took it	Problems I had	Suggestions
a ...*telesales*...	*Interested*		*Si ... phone*
b *sales assistant*	*learn*	*long-hours*	*flexible*
c			
d			
e			

2 Choose one of the jobs a–e and write an answer to the task in 150 words.

ORGANISE YOUR POINTS LOGICALLY AND CLEARLY

You can use the bullet points in the task as a basic paragraph plan for your letter. Then you need to think about how to organise the points in each paragraph.

- Read this example of a GT Writing task.

  Last week you went to a musical concert. You were very impressed with the performance.

  Write a letter to a friend about the concert. In your letter
  - *say what the concert was and why you went*
  - *describe the performance*
  - *suggest why he/she should go to the concert*

3 Look at these notes. Put the remaining points in the order in which you think they should be described in a letter.

Good for all ages
Well-known songs
Very unusual
Finishes next Monday
South African singers
No musical instruments
Mum's birthday
'The Swing Band'
One-hour performance

a Mother's b'day
b SA singers
c The Swing Band
  ↓
d ....
e ....
f ....
  ↓
g ....
h ....
i ....

85

TEST TIP

You do not have to respond to the bullet points in the same order as they are presented. The important thing is to cover all the points in a logical order.

• Read this sample paragraph.

> 'Last week I went to see a musical concert and I was very impressed with the performance. It was a group from South Africa. Their name was 'The Swing Band'. My mother came. It was her birthday.'

4 The paragraph contains all the content points and there are no grammatical mistakes. However, there are two reasons why it would still lose marks. What are they?

5 Can you rewrite the paragraph so that you would not lose marks?

6 Here is a different answer to the same task. What notes did the writer work with? Complete the notes below.

> Dear Katy,
> I must tell you about the concert that I went to see last Monday. I hadn't intended to go but my neighbour offered me a spare ticket for this Brazilian percussion band called 'Hot Jive'. As I had nothing planned for the evening, I agreed to go.
> As a spectacle, the whole evening was amazing. The players wore the most beautiful, brightly-coloured clothes and the scenery changed as the evening progressed from sunrise, at the start, to sunset at the end of the show. In terms of the music, the most memorable part was a fifteen-minute number called 'Jungle Rhythms', which, as the name suggests, incorporated lots of animal sounds that were made using drums and many other weird and wonderful instruments.
> I know from the programme that I bought during the interval that they will be playing in your town next month and I really recommend that you go. You may think drums are loud and boring but wait till you hear this!

- ticket from neighbour
- ....
- ....
- ....
- ....
- ....
- ....

IELTS Writing (GT)	**Task 1**

🕐 20

TEST TIP

Use your own experience to give you ideas, if you can, but don't be afraid to make things up if you need to.

You recently visited a place that had a strong impact on you.

Write a letter to a friend about the place. In your letter
- *explain where the place was and how you got there*
- *describe what you saw*
- *offer to take your friend there*

You should write at least 150 words.

Writing

UNIT 6 General Training, Task 1 continued

GET YOUR MESSAGE ACROSS

Your examiner will be looking for a clear message in your letter. Think carefully about what language to use so that the reason you are writing and the response you want are clear to the examiner.

- Read this task.

   For the past six months you have provided voluntarily help at a local school for 5–7 year-olds. Unfortunately you can no longer do this work.

   Write a letter to the principal of the school. In your letter
   - *explain what you have been doing at the school*
   - *give reasons why you can no longer do the work*
   - *apologise for any problems this may cause*

1 Which words in the task indicate the purpose of the letter?

2 Which part of the task does this sample extract address? How is this part different from the other parts?

> Please accept my apologies for bringing you this news. I sincerely hope that you are able to find a replacement for me without too much difficulty.

3 Read the following extracts from letters and underline the words in each letter that indicate the writer's purpose.

a

> I cannot understand why someone with less experience than myself has been appointed to this post.

b

> I have three years' experience in sales and I feel confident I would make a positive contribution to your team.

c

> We greatly appreciate the help that you gave our son during his music exams.

d

> We wonder whether it would be possible to visit your company on September 6th as our class is very interested in the whole area of software publications.

e

> Although there were plenty of staff at the swimming pool, I did not feel sure that they were paying enough attention to what was going on.

f

> Despite the fact that I have written a letter and made several calls to your reception desk, I still find I am being sent a monthly bill for membership fees.

g

> Mike played the guitar beautifully at the concert and we were all very impressed by the general standard of the school's orchestra.

4 Match the extracts to these possible reasons for writing a letter.

- **i** to make a polite enquiry
- **ii** to show gratitude for support
- **iii** to request financial help
- **iv** to show dissatisfaction with a decision
- **v** to explain why something happened
- **vi** to express pleasure at an event
- **vii** to support a job application
- **viii** to ask for an apology
- **ix** to express concern about safety
- **x** to complain about a service

5 Write a short paragraph that responds to each of these situations. Invent information to support your reason for writing.

- **a** You hear your neighbour's car stereo every night. Give him/her a good reason to turn it down, e.g. your baby.
- **b** Remind your Aunt Helen about your graduation next month – you really want her to come.
- **c** Tell Mrs Fry at JBC company you enjoyed meeting her and that you will be working together a lot next year.
- **d** Apologise to Sue about forgetting her birthday. Send her some theatre tickets.
- **e** You are fed up with your employees: they must lock the garage door, or there will be a burglary.
- **f** Thank Alex for the loan of his video camera – you got some great shots.

- Swap paragraphs with your study partner and say whether the structures used communicated the message successfully.

SET THE RIGHT TONE

- You need to use appropriate language in your letter to give it the right tone – formal, neutral or informal.

6 Read the messages you wrote in 5 and say what tone you used.

7 Read this GT Task 1 and the three possible opening paragraphs below. Decide which of them is the most appropriate and why.

> *You recently bought a computer from a reputable computer store. The store agreed to deliver the computer and set it up for you in your home but when it was delivered, the delivery man claimed that this was not part of his job.*
>
> *Write a letter to the manager of the store. In your letter*
> * *say when you bought the computer and what the price included*
> * *express dissatisfaction about what has occurred*
> * *find out what they intend to do about it.*

a

I am very unhappy about the fact that your store agreed to deliver my new computer and set it up for me in my home but when it was delivered, your delivery man claimed that this was not part of his job. I'm afraid I didn't believe him and this just isn't good enough.

TEST TIP

You do not always need to 'complain' when you are giving factual details that support a complaint.

b

On 3rd May I purchased a 'Riteway' personal computer from your city store. The price of $2,500 included delivery and set up in my home, and I attach a copy of the receipt. However, when it was delivered yesterday, the delivery man was quite unaware of the agreement and left without setting up the computer for me.

c

I am writing to express my disgust with the service provided by your store. The store promised to set up my new computer at home for me but this has not occurred and you have not fulfilled your contract.

8 What, if anything, is wrong with the two options that you did not choose?

9 Now complete the letter by writing two more paragraphs plus a closing sentence.

IELTS Writing (GT)	Task 1

⏱ 20

> *For the past year you have been a member of a local club. Now you want to discontinue your membership.*
>
> *Write a letter to the club secretary. In your letter*
> * *state what type of membership you have and how you have paid for this*
> * *give details of how you have benefited from the club*
> * *explain why you want to leave*

You should write at least 150 words.

Writing

In Writing Task 2, marks are awarded for the ideas and arguments that you include in your answer. It is, therefore, important to spend at least five minutes analysing the task, forming ideas and deciding how you will develop these, before you begin writing.

ANALYSE THE TASK

IELTS Writing Tasks have a range of formats but you are always expected to produce a written discussion of the topic.

- Read this GT Task 2.

    Task A

    In achieving personal happiness, our relationships with other people (family, friends, colleagues) are more important than anything else. Issues such as work and wealth take second place.

    Do you agree or disagree?

The discussion topic is presented to you as a one-sided statement. You can support the statement, you can argue against it, or you can do both. Here are some questions that may help you decide how you would approach Task A.

- Do you agree with the statement? Why?

1 Which of the words in the task will help you develop your main ideas?
2 How useful is the information in brackets?
3 Are there any important 'issues' that you think have been left out of this question?
4 Is this a philosophical question or a practical question? Is there one correct answer?
5 Can you turn the whole task into a question?

- Here is a different task that presents both sides of an argument.

    Task B

    Some people argue that there are no fundamental differences between the way men and women approach academic study. Others insist that there are big differences in areas such as organisation, attitude and ambition, and that these differences inevitably have an impact on student life.

    What are your opinions on this?

- Do you agree with one of the views presented in the task or do you think there are arguments for both?

6 Which of the words in the task will help you develop your main ideas?

7 Is this a general question about the differences between men and women?

8 How might the wording of the question help you organise your answer?

9 Do you have to organise your answer in this way?

FORMING IDEAS – ONE IDEA IS NOT ENOUGH!

In order to write an essay of 250 words or more, you need to have several main ideas which you can then organise into paragraphs and develop using supporting points and examples.

- Read this paragraph from a sample essay on Task A (page 90).

> Paragraph a
> In my opinion my friends are the most important people in my life. This is because my friends are more important to me than anyone else and they help me in my life. Actually I have a lot of friends and I feel very lucky to have so many friends. Other people may not have good friends but I would not be happy without my friends around. Even if I am ill, I still need my friends and no one else can take their place. As a consequence, I value them very highly.

10 What is the main idea of the paragraph?

11 What are the supporting points?

12 What do you notice about the language that is used?

13 How could this paragraph be improved?

In terms of structure, Paragraph a looks something like this:

In my opinion my friends are the most important people in my life. This is because...

TEST TIP
If you repeat your words or ideas too much in the test, you will lose marks.

TEST TIP
You are advised to read as widely as possible in order to develop your views and ideas on a range of well-known topics.

- Read this paragraph from a sample essay on Task B (page 90).

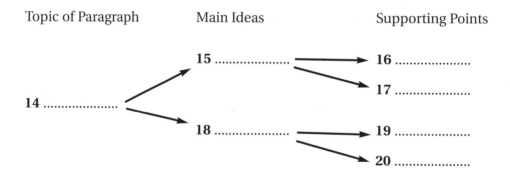

Paragraph b
It has always seemed to me that men organise their study time in a different way from women. In my experience, men are more likely to study on their own, whereas women prefer to work in groups and to agree certain principles about their assignments together. Obviously not everyone behaves in the same way but in my country, these patterns of behaviour are common. Also, in terms of time management, women generally have a more realistic view of how long certain tasks will take. Men, on the other hand, are prone to under-estimating the length of time they need for something and can end up spending a lot longer than anticipated.

- Using the structure diagram below, extract the main ideas and the supporting points from Paragraph b.

Topic of Paragraph   Main Ideas   Supporting Points

15 .... ────────→ 16 ....

                                                        17 ....

14 ....

18 .... ────────→ 19 ....

                                                        20 ....

- Now rewrite Paragraph a on page 91. Make a small plan first, then take no more than 15 minutes to write your paragraph.

 - Exchange your paragraph with your study partner and see whether you can identify each other's main ideas and supporting points.

- Refer to *Insight into IELTS* pages 83–84, for more guidance on forming ideas.

Writing

In addition to receiving marks for the content of your Task 2 answer, you will also receive marks for producing a clear, convincing argument and/or description. This means that your ideas should be presented in a logical sequence.

UNDERSTAND THE DIFFERENCE BETWEEN MAIN AND SUPPORTING IDEAS

- Read the following task and the sample answer, then answer the questions below.

> *People who have original ideas are of much greater value to society than those who are simply able to copy the ideas of others well.*
>
> *To what extent do you agree or disagree with this statement?*

I certainly agree that people who come up with new ideas; in other words those who 'invent' or 'discover' things are terribly important to society as a whole. However, I also think there is a role in society for good imitators.

No one would deny that key individuals must be thanked for providing us with certain facilities that we use every day. Where would we be, for example, without basic items such as the washing machine, the television and, more recently, the computer? These items are now used so regularly that we tend to take them for granted.

In fact, the society we live in today has become increasingly consumer-oriented, and while it may be possible to constantly update and improve consumer goods, not everyone where I live can afford the prices of these innovations. Furthermore, not everyone lives in

an area that has accessibility to the latest models on the market. For this reason, there is a value to be placed on being able to provide good copies of expensive items.

Having said that, certain innovations have a more serious impact on our lives than consumer goods and cannot easily be replicated. Vital medicines like penicillin and vaccines against dangerous diseases also exist because people made continual efforts to develop them. Scientific ideas such as these enable us to live longer and escape illness.

Undoubtedly, scientists and engineers work extremely hard to make life better for us. In some areas, their work adds comfort to our lives, and if people copy their ideas it helps a wider population to benefit from them. However, in other areas, their contribution is unique, cannot be copied and without it we would be unlikely to survive or move forward.

1 How does the writer respond to the task in the introduction?
How does the writer use paragraphing to develop the answer?
Underline the main idea in paragraphs 2, 3 and 4.
Underline a supporting point in each paragraph.
Do you think the writer's answer has a clear line of development?
How useful is the conclusion?

THE BODY

The body of an essay consists of two or more paragraphs, each with a clear set of ideas.

- Read this task and the ideas below.

   In order to be able to study well, students need an attractive, clean learning environment. Universities and Colleges should make efforts to provide this.

   Discuss.

- Organise the ideas using the structure diagram below to help.

Para 2   **Supporting points**

Main idea   2 ....

Why might a clean   3 ....

environment help?   4 ....

Para 3

Main idea   5 ....

Compare education   6 ....

with other areas of life   7 ....

Para 3

Main idea   8 ....

Is it the main responsibility   9 ....

of a university?   10 ....

The order you present the points in each paragraph will depend partly on what emphasis you want to give and what language you choose. These points will be covered in the next unit.

THE INTRODUCTION AND THE CONCLUSION

11 Read this task and the sample introductions and conclusions. Say whether a, b, c
    and d are introductions or conclusions. Discuss the reasons for your choice with
    your study partner.

> *Crime is nearly always related to the environment in which it occurs. For this*
> *reason, international laws and international law courts are unrealistic and*
> *will not succeed in reducing crime levels in different countries.*
>
> *Discuss.*

a Initially, the argument seems reasonable, but in order to verify this, a closer examination of the principles behind it is needed.

c Thus while the theory behind the establishment of international laws seems a good one, it has to be said that such a system would be unlikely to work in practice.

b Taking all the arguments into account, it seems that there is substantial evidence to show a link between crime and the location in which it occurs.

d Is there a relationship between crime and the environment, and, if there is, is it justifiable to jump to the conclusion that international laws will not work?

• Practise writing some *introductory* sentences. Look at the task on the previous
  page and write one or two sentences that

12 generally agree with the statement.

13 express some doubt about the statement.

14 express a mixed view on the statement.

15 question the definition of 'study well'.

16 explain what you understand by 'environment'.

TEST TIP

Remember that you must not copy from the task itself. Always try to re-phrase the information in the question by using your own words.

IELTS Writing	**Task 2**

Pre-task questions

• Ask yourself some questions about the task in order to understand it fully and
  decide how you would like to address it.

• Map out some ideas on the task using a structure diagram.

• Write an answer to the task and time yourself. You should aim to take less than 40
  minutes to write it as you have already spent some time preparing your answer.

> You should spend about 40 minutes on this task.
> Present a written argument or case to an educated reader with no specialist
> knowledge of the following topic.
>
> *In some countries, marriages are arranged by the parents but in other cases,*
> *people choose their own marriage partner.*
>
> *Discuss both systems.*
>
> You should use your own ideas, knowledge and experience and support your
> arguments with examples and relevant evidence.

Writing

Your ability to *communicate* your ideas will depend partly on good planning. However, it will also depend on the language that you use to introduce and develop your argument. This will be covered in the next two units.

USE APPROPRIATE STRUCTURES

Your examiner will be looking for a range of language and an appropriate use of sentence structures. For example, you may make a forceful statement about your views starting, e.g. *I firmly believe that...* , or generalise your argument by using *Most people would argue that...* .
Or you could admit there are positive aspects to the topic but still argue against it on a personal level, e.g. *Despite... , I still feel...* .

- Match statements 1–10 with the ways of introducing arguments a–h.

1 *On the whole, people tend to feel that* human nature is fundamentally good.

2 *While I appreciate* the importance of computers, *I still think* we rely too heavily on them nowadays.

3 *Do* film stars *need to be paid* such high salaries?

4 *It is inevitable that* human cloning *will* one day become a reality.

5 In this context, *it is appropriate to assume that* 'professional expertise' *refers to* the skill with which people do their jobs.

6 *I am not convinced that* goal setting is a critical aspect of personal fulfilment.

7 *There is every reason to predict that* the quality of healthcare *will* continue to decline in this country.

8 *Regardless of* the costs involved, *it is always worth* hiring the best people.

9 *Overall*, people *have a tendency to* resist change.

10 Children *are similar to* animals *in* their need to be cared for and loved.

a by making a comparison/contrast	**e** by refuting an argument
b by making a concession	**f** by giving a definition/clarification
c by generalising	**g** by expressing doubt
d by making a prediction/speculating	**h** by asking a rhetorical question

- Decide how the writer might continue the argument in each statement.

RHETORICAL QUESTIONS

Look at this rhetorical question from paragraph 2 on page 93.

Where would we be, for example, without basic items such as the washing machine, the television and, more recently, the computer?

Rhetorical questions are a common feature of academic writing. They are used because they add emphasis to a point, and they do not require an answer.

• Make the following statements into rhetorical questions using the question word given.

11 There is no crime more shocking than cold-blooded murder. (What?)

12 I can't understand why anyone would want to go to prison. (Why?)

13 Big cities have the highest crime rates. (Where?)

14 It is impossible to compare a crime in one country with the same crime in another. (How?)

15 It is impossible to say how long someone should spend in prison. (Who?)

USE APPROPRIATE AND PRECISE LANGUAGE

When you have an idea, it is important to think about what you really mean and how it might be best to express that idea in writing. Imagine that this is one of your main ideas.

We wouldn't buy so many things if advertisements didn't exist.

The idea is relevant but it can be expressed more appropriately. If you decide that a rhetorical question would be a better way to introduce the idea, think about how to turn the sentence into a question, e.g.

'Would we buy so many (things) if advertisements did not (exist)?'

You also need to think about the words you use. 'Things' is not a very precise word. 'Products' or 'luxury goods' would be more precise. Also 'exist' is used to refer to living creatures; advertisements are 'produced' by marketing companies or 'shown' by TV advertising companies. With thought, your idea could look a lot better:

Would we buy so many luxury goods, if marketing companies didn't produce so many advertisements?

or

Would we buy so many goods if we were shown fewer advertisements?

or

Without advertising, would we buy so many products?

TEST TIP

Your examiner will be looking for appropriate structures and precise vocabulary. You will lose marks if your ideas are vague and poorly expressed.

- Read the following sample extracts. Using the prompts improve the way the main idea is introduced. Work with your study partner, if you can.

16 We just accept mobile phones and don't think about their bad effects.

have a tendency / regardless of

17 It's not right that parents can choose if they have a boy or girl baby.

my view / is unethical for

18 A lot of steps have been taken to help old people but it's still not enough.

Despite the fact that / we still

19 I think a lot of people don't know the effect of antibiotics.

doubtful whether many

20 People say that hamburgers make you fat but it isn't true.

little evidence to

21 Some people say they want to work at home which I find surprising.

always surprised when

- Now decide for yourself the best way of expressing the following ideas. There is no correct answer, although some structures will be more appropriate than others.

22 Fake designer watches seem fine to me.

23 Most young children play too many computer games these days.

24 One day we'll realise that it's no good to cut down so many trees.

25 It's true that some children's stories are scary but they still like to read them.

26 I don't think teams are as good in business as just one person.

27 I describe someone as 'fit' if they do regular exercise.

EXPRESSING FEELINGS

> Feelings and reactions can be expressed by combining adverbs and adjectives with other phrases/structures, e.g. *I am frequently surprised to learn...* , *People are rarely shocked by...* .

- Read this sentence which uses a negative adverb to communicate strong feelings. It tells the reader that, in your opinion, it is perfectly understandable that young people might be undecided about their careers.

I am never surprised to hear young people say they have yet to decide on a career.

A 'double negative' format is also used to give emphasis to an unexpected situation.

It is not	unusual uncommon impossible	for (+ object + infinitive)	*It is quite usual...* *It is quite common...* *It is quite possible...*
	inconceivable	that	*There is a slight possibility...*

• Write sentences to express the following ideas using structures from the table.

28 Tourists may be able to take a holiday on the moon in the next decade.

29 Children can often do simple sums by the age of five.

30 Women can do a full-time job, look after children and run a home.

31 Well-established painters sometimes decide to change from one medium to another.

• Read this short essay on the topic of water conservation.

> The writer has lost marks because the answer is very short, the language is repetitive and the structures and introductory clauses are inappropriate.

> Everybody knows that water is a very important thing because we need water for everything we do.
>
> Our bodies are made up of 70% water and we need it to drink, and to wash, and to grow things.
>
> As far as I am concerned, we should do more to save our water and not waste it. Because every drop counts. Regarding water conservation, the government should not store water in large dams as much of it evaporates and is lost into the atmosphere. There is also recycling.
>
> These are the reasons why water is important.

32 Rewrite the answer.

   a Identify the main idea in each paragraph and rewrite it using an appropriate structure.

   b Think of some more supporting points for the main idea, and if you can, reinforce one or two of the main ideas.

   c Write an introduction and a conclusion for the essay.

• Refer to *Insight into IELTS* pages 88–90 for more useful language and structures.

TEST TIP

Don't overuse the structures in this unit. If you include too many, and/or use them inappropriately, they will detract from the communicative quality of your answer and you will lose marks.

Writing

Once you have written your main argument clearly, you then need to support it in an appropriate way. Remember that your support must be relevant to the argument and sufficient to develop the argument.

STRUCTURE YOUR ARGUMENT CAREFULLY

A paragraph in the body of an essay usually consists of a main idea and its supporting arguments, (although there are variations on this and sometimes more than one main idea is presented in a paragraph).

- Here is an IELTS Task 2 followed by some notes for one paragraph in the essay.

It has been suggested that in the not-too-distant future, people will take their holidays on the moon. How realistic do you think this is?

What type of holidays do you think people will take in the future?

Moon holidays? → Cost
→ Dangers
→ Facilities

- Read this paragraph from the body of a sample answer.

a

What about moon holidays? I don't think it's very possible for three reasons. Firstly it will be very expensive to travel in space. Secondly it is dangerous. You might not come back. Thirdly, there aren't many facilities in space. For all these reasons, I think people won't choose to go on holiday in space.

1 How has the writer linked the supporting points to the main idea?

2 Are the linking devices appropriate?

3 What is the function of the final sentence?

4 Identify three ways that the writer could improve on this paragraph, e.g. content, choice of vocabulary, etc.

• Here is another paragraph on the same topic, using the same notes.

b

> I would predict that it is unlikely that people will choose to go to the moon for their holiday in the future. Who would want to travel to the moon? Actually, it would be very expensive to do this and some people can't afford it. Besides, there are a lot of dangerous aspects to it and people may be afraid. On the other hand, the facilities would be limited and people would prefer to be at home.

5 How has the writer linked the supporting points to the main idea?

6 Are the linking devices appropriate?

7 Is the rhetorical question appropriate here?

8 Identify three ways that the student could improve on this paragraph.

• Read this paragraph which would receive very good marks despite the few mistakes. Then answer questions 9–13 to analyse why it is so successful.

c

one

would be able to

duration

> According to space experts, some people will soon be so eager to try something new that they will happily check into a moon hotel – assuming (it) is available. As far as I am concerned, this is a rather far-fetched idea. To begin with, the cost of travelling to the moon is likely to be so high that only the extremely wealthy (can) afford it. Secondly, though it is argued that tourists are looking for a challenge, the dangers involved in just getting to the moon are well known and these will surely put a lot of people off the idea. Besides, even if you do manage to get up there safely, you still have to survive in an alien atmosphere for the (time) of the holiday. And lastly, what will tourists do in space? Can you imagine playing space football, for example?

9 Why is the opening sentence better than those used in the other two paragraphs?

10 What do you notice about the choice of vocabulary?

11 Underline the linking words and structures. Are they varied and appropriate?

12 What does 'besides' mean? What is it used to link?

13 Why do you think the writer chose to use a rhetorical question at the end?

USE A RANGE OF LINKERS

> There are a variety of ways in which supporting points can be linked to a main idea or extended as ideas themselves. In paragraph c, the writer sequenced the points using phrases (*to begin with*) and adverbs (*secondly, lastly*). There is also a variety of other linking words and phrases used which successfully structure her answer.

- Now look at this set of notes that a different writer made for *two* paragraphs on the same topic.

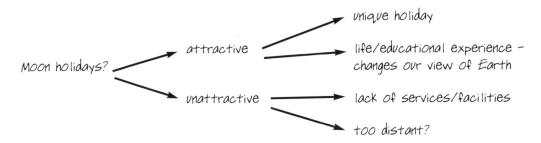

14 What structures might the student use to express the main points in the two paragraphs?

15 What experience might the second supporting point relate to?

16 How might the student develop the third supporting point?

- Look at the following skeleton of the two paragraphs.

As far as I can see, ... On the one hand, ... in that .... not only .... but also .... As films have repeatedly shown, ...

On the other hand, ... For those who are concerned about .... such as .... or .... Ultimately, isn't .... People are still reluctant to .... ; they are unlikely to ....

- Can you state the function of all the linkers in this skeleton?

17 Complete the paragraphs by writing in the main and supporting points using the notes above.

- Here is a third set of notes for the same task. This writer has chosen to question the feasibility of moon holidays.

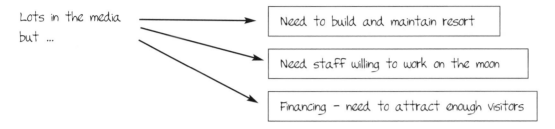

Lots in the media but ...

Need to build and maintain resort

Need staff willing to work on the moon

Financing – need to attract enough visitors

18 Write a paragraph using these notes. Use appropriate linkers and a concessional structure. Take about 10 minutes.

| **IELTS Writing** | **TASK 2** |

- Take five minutes to plan an answer to the task. Think about the structures that you will use and the relevant vocabulary. Write your answer in 35 minutes.

  You should spend about 40 minutes on this task.

  Present a written argument or case to an educated reader with no specialist knowledge of the following topic.

  According to those in the travel business, the nature of the average 'holiday' is changing. Rather than seeking a relaxing break in a far-away place, people now want excitement on their holidays and are keen to participate in unusual and challenging activities.

  Do you agree or disagree?

  You should use your own ideas, knowledge and experience and support your arguments with examples and relevant evidence.

Writing

In writing your answer to Task 1 and Task 2, it is important to develop ideas and plan your answer; use appropriate structures to introduce points or arguments; and develop your answer with relevant information or ideas.

It is also important to write coherently (link points within and between sentences well), and write clearly and accurately, demonstrating a range of vocabulary and sentence structures.

WHAT MAKES A COHERENT ANSWER?

- Re-read the beginning of a sample paragraph on moon holidays and the notes around it.

Good examples of complex sentences.

What does this linker mean?

I would question whether so-called 'moon holidays' are ever likely to be possible. Although the media frequently reports on things like the building of moon hotels and provides images of a typical moon holiday resort, I doubt whether these are anything more than speculative. Even if it is possible to construct and encapsulate an atmosphere on the moon that can sustain human life, how practical is it going to be to maintain this? Are those involved in...

What do these words refer to?

- Using the words in the box below to help, rewrite the following sets of sentences to make them more coherent.

1 I think most people get nervous about giving a speech. Most people lose their nerves once they get started.

2 I tend to disagree with the popular view that music is beneficial to children. It's true that children like music. But I don't think they need to learn it at school. Does it use up valuable time that should be spent on other activities?

3 Libraries are marvellous places. They need to improve their image. Many people find them boring.

4 Smoking among young people has dropped by 2% over the last two years. There has been an effective anti-smoking campaign. Cigarettes are expensive.

5 Global warming is a reality. There is no real evidence of climatic change. Changes in climate have been a feature of the Earth's history.

while	even (if / though)	as a result of
to make matters worse	not only...but also	in that
having said that	however	in addition

HOW CAN YOU IMPROVE YOUR USE OF VOCABULARY?

Remember that you need to be clear and precise in your use of vocabulary. If you try to use the vocabulary that you already know as *fully and appropriately as possible*, you will begin to achieve this.

Use more adjectives and adverbs

Here are some phrases from the paragraphs on moon holidays on pages 101 and 104. In describing ideas, actions, people and places, the writer has made use of adverbs and adjectives to add precision to what is said.

'happily check into'
'rather far-fetched idea'
'the extremely wealthy'
'alien atmosphere'
'frequently reports'
'typical moon holidays'

TEST TIP
Avoid words like very, nice, OK, good, lovely, when writing. Try to use more precise words.

105

In Writing Task 2, you often discuss ideas and opinions. 'Far-fetched' can be used to describe what you think is a ridiculous idea. In the boxes below there are some other words that can be used when describing opinions.

- Make these nouns into noun phrases by selecting an adjective to go with each noun.

Adjectives	Nouns
unhelpful / helpful	idea
old-fashioned / current	view
unrealistic / realistic	suggestion
negative / positive	claim
one-sided / impartial	comment
unpopular / popular	point
pessimistic / optimistic	argument

- Try adding an adverb to your phrases; e.g. 'totally', 'absolutely', 'quite', 'rather', 'fairly'.

Develop your use of prefixes and suffixes

In order to make wider and better use of the vocabulary that you already know, you need to use prefixes and suffixes. For example, to make the adjective *sufficient* (meaning 'enough') into an adverb that means 'not enough', you need to do the following:

Prefix	Stem	Suffix
in	*sufficient*	*ly*

You can then make a statement such as, 'People are insufficiently motivated to take part in political debate these days'.

- Improve the following sentences by replacing the italicised words with an appropriate adverb or adjective from the word in brackets. Make sure you understand when to use an adverb or an adjective.

6 The market is expanding *so much all the time*. (*rapid*)

7 *More and more* numbers of women are going out to work. (*increase*)

8 This book is *so good it's better than all the others*. (*exception*)

9 I *made a mistake and* bought the wrong size shoes. (*mistaken*)

10 People argue *over and over again* that violence on television is harmful. (*repeat*)

11 The number of people who work at home has increased *three times over*. (*three*)

12 Country A's exports are *a lot* higher than country B's. (*consider*)

Choose the 'best' word(s)

> The accuracy of your answer depends not only on your grammatical knowledge but also on your choice of vocabulary. You will make fewer mistakes in your writing if you leave time at the end of the test to proof-read your own answer.

- Read this sample answer and improve it by using more precise words. Use the notes to help you.

Young children go to school for a number of reasons: not only to learn <u>useful</u> skills such as reading, writing and mathematics, but also to learn how to get on with each other. In other words, the <u>acquiring</u> of social skills is <u>also</u> important.

One of the <u>best</u> ways to teach young children how to work together is to get them to <u>do</u> music together, particularly music which involves percussion instruments such as drums and symbols. These are instruments which do not require <u>much</u> skill to play and which children seem to enjoy <u>a lot</u>. Learning to play music together teaches them the skill of co-operation which does not always come <u>happily</u> to young children.

Children can be introduced to <u>music</u> concepts like pitch and rhythm <u>by</u> a number of activities: dancing, singing and playing instruments are all <u>good</u> and enjoyable. In this way they become familiar with music and, if well guided, go on to enjoy all kinds of music <u>for</u> the rest of their lives.

Notes – suggestions

They are more than useful?

Noun from the verb acquire?
Different adverb.

Be more precise.
Find another verb.

Find another way to say this.

Adverb?
Include an adjective before 'skill'.
Find a better adverb.

Adjective from music?
Preposition?

Find a more precise adjective.

Preposition which indicates a long time.

TEST TIP
Remember that grammar, punctuation and spelling are also very important. It is a good idea to keep a record of the common mistakes that you make and check for these every time you do some writing.

107

Speaking

Part 1	The interview	4–5 mins
Part 2	Individual long turn	
Part 3	Two-way discussion	

UNIT 1 Part one of the Speaking test – the interview

Part 1 of the test lasts four to five minutes. The examiner will introduce himself or herself to you and ask you for your name and some photo identification. You will then be asked to talk about some familiar topics. The examiner will ask a number of questions to which you should reply as fully as possible.

BECOMING MORE FLUENT

One way of improving your overall fluency – that is your ability to keep going – is to answer questions by always providing some extra information and linking this information to your first response.

- Match these questions to the responses in the box below.

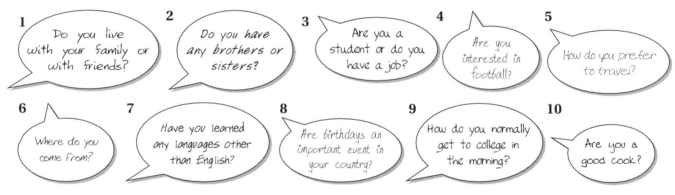

1 Do you live with your family or with friends?

2 Do you have any brothers or sisters?

3 Are you a student or do you have a job?

4 Are you interested in football?

5 How do you prefer to travel?

6 Where do you come from?

7 Have you learned any languages other than English?

8 Are birthdays an important event in your country?

9 How do you normally get to college in the morning?

10 Are you a good cook?

a No – not at all. In fact I'm not very interested in any kind of sport, to be honest with you.

b I like the train because you can see out of the window or read a book … but sometimes you have to fly because of the distances involved.

c I'm from a small village in the mountains – a long way from the capital city of my country.

d I'm a student but I do have a part time job to help support myself.

e Yes, I have. I studied Spanish at school although I don't remember very much now.

f Yes, they are, and it's customary to share a cake or give a card or present .

g No – I'm a only child. I have ten cousins that I grew up with, so I didn't ever feel lonely.

h Well … I enjoy trying out new recipes. And nobody has complained yet!

i Actually, I'm staying in a university hall of residence as I'm an overseas student studying here for a year.

j I take the train to Central Station and then I catch the express bus – it takes about an hour altogether.

- There are at least two parts to each of the responses a to j on page 108. Read the responses again and underline any words which link the response to the original question. Say whether the link is:

  a a vocabulary link, i.e. a link through meaning
  b a grammatical link, i.e. a conjunction, a relative pronoun

The first one has been done for you below.

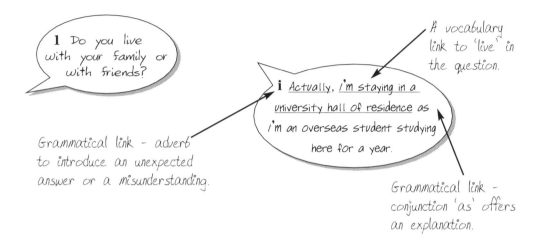

1 Do you live with your family or with friends?

i Actually, I'm staying in a university hall of residence as I'm an overseas student studying here for a year.

A vocabulary link to 'live' in the question.

Grammatical link – adverb to introduce an unexpected answer or a misunderstanding.

Grammatical link – conjunction 'as' offers an explanation.

LINKING YOUR IDEAS

- Work with your study partner and ask each other all the questions in the speech bubbles on page 108 and give your own answers. If possible, record your answers.

- Make sure you give *two* pieces of information in each of your answers and try linking them together. Did you find any new ways of linking your ideas?

- If you managed to record your answers, draw up a table like the one below and then listen to your recording and try to complete the table based on your responses.

Additional info	Linking words
a not very interested in any kind of sport	in fact

GUIDED SPEAKING – TALKING ABOUT WHERE YOU GREW UP

EXTRACT 1

- You will hear two people talking about where they grew up. As you listen, look at the main and additional information which has been completed for the first speaker in the table below.

- Listen to the second speaker and complete the table with similar information. Listen as many times as you wish.

First speaker

	Main information	Additional information
Name of place	Victoria	Capital of British Columbia, Canada
Location	Vancouver Island	Vancouver not on Vancouver Island
Good points	Good climate Lovely architecture Eco-tourism – whale watching Popular destination	Better than Eastern Canada –– Best from May to Sept Safe, clean, friendly
Closing words	Visit the Butchart Gardens	Even if you don't like gardens

Second speaker

	Main information	Additional information
Name of place		
Location		
Good points		
Closing words		

- Work with your study partner. Take it in turns to tell each other about the place where you grew up. Make sure you give a number of important pieces of information followed by a supporting point or two. Try to end with an interesting or humorous point.
- While your partner is talking, show that you are listening, by maintaining eye contact.
- When your partner has finished speaking, complete the grid below together.

Your partner

	Main information	Additional information
Name of place		
Location		
Good points		
Closing words		

TEST TIP

During the speaking test it is important to speak directly to the examiner. Don't be afraid to maintain eye contact – it is very natural in the English-speaking world.

PRONUNCIATION PRACTICE – SENTENCE STRESS

 EXTRACT 2

Because English is spoken in so many different parts of the world, there are many different accents in English, and the pronunciation of individual words and sounds may vary from one country to another. Generally speaking, however, the varieties spoken by educated native speakers follow the same overall patterns of stress and intonation.

- Listen to Speaking Unit 1 Extract 2, the opening sentences spoken by the Canadian woman. Note how it takes the same amount of time to say the words in each box, although there are more words in some boxes than others. This is because English is a time stressed language.

I grew	**up** in a	**cit**y called Vic	**tor**ia.	
It's the	**cap**ital of the	**State** of British Co	**lum**bia in	**Can**ada.

- Listen to how the woman says the words below and underline where the stress falls.

  'Victoria has a pretty good climate... usually quite warm and certainly much better than the eastern states of Canada.'

- Look at these sentences and practise saying them to yourself. Work out where the stress is likely to fall. Then listen again and check.

  'I think it's a great place to grow up... not too big, not too small with some really lovely architecture.'

  'And the island itself is just so beautiful, once you get out of the city, that is.'

  'I think Victoria is popular, predominantly because it's safe... clean... and, of course, the people are very friendly.'

PRONUNCIATION PRACTICE – WORDS

 EXTRACT 3

- Listen to these words again and note which syllables the speaker stresses. Practise repeating the words to yourself.

island	popular	whale watching	breathtakingly
climate	restaurants	wide streets	predominantly
architecture	friendly	a European feel	certainly
19th century architecture	rivalry	eco-tourism	incredibly

Speaking

Part 1	The interview	4–5 mins
Part 2	Individual long turn	
Part 3	Two-way discussion	

UNIT 2 More practice for Part one

When the examiner asks you a question in Part 1, make sure you answer that question. Don't just start talking on any topic. Listen for the key words in the question which carry essential meaning – they may be nouns or verbs.

- **What are the key words in this question?**

> What kind of music do you like?

> I really like rock music. These days you can find a lot of good music on the Internet. And that's fantastic!

> I really only listen to classical music and opera. To be honest with you, I find modern music quite unbearable. It's just a terrible noise as far as I'm concerned.

> Actually, my favourite kind of music is film music. I enjoy listening to the sound tracks of movies - especially when I've really enjoyed the film.

WAYS OF ANSWERING QUESTIONS

 EXTRACT 1

- Read and listen to the three responses and answer these questions.

1 Which of the speakers relies most on the wording of the question to construct an answer?

2 How many additional pieces of information does each of the speakers provide?

3 Why does the girl start with the word 'actually'?

4 What does the woman really mean by 'To be honest with you...'? What other expression does she use?

- Try to think of two more ways of answering this question about music. Be inventive and always provide some additional information.

112

- Now look at the questions below. Underline the key words in each question.

- For each question, write an answer which includes the key words. If you wish, use one of the opening expressions in the box below. Make sure you choose one which makes an appropriate response to the question.

What is the best way to learn how to use a computer?

What is your favourite meal of the day?

What do you want to do when you finish this course?

What time of the year do you like best?

What sort of TV programmes do you enjoy watching?

Do you prefer to study in a library or at home?

How do you like to spend your spare time?

Would you prefer to get an e-mail message or a letter?

What kind of music do you like?

Does it matter to you what kind of clothes people wear? Do you judge people by their clothes?

Do you like learning in groups or alone?

Do you often go to the cinema? What sort of films do you normally choose to watch?

Generally speaking I …
On the whole I …
I tend to prefer …
I'm not very keen on …

TEST TIP

Make sure your answer is relevant to the question.

113

GUIDED SPEAKING – TALKING ABOUT A SPORT

 EXTRACT 2

- Listen to Speaking Unit 2 Extract 2. You will hear two people talking about a sport they enjoy playing. As you listen, look at the main and additional information for the first speaker in the table.

- Listen to the second speaker and complete the table with similar information. You may listen as many times as you wish.

First speaker

	Main information	Additional information
Sport	Skiing	Started at age six
Tough things	Dangerous – broken bones common	Knee injuries Hit trees / get lost
Good things	Solitude Challenging	Sense of freedom
Closing words	It beats any team sport, in my opinion	

Second speaker

	Main information	Additional information
Sport		
Tough things		
Good things		
Closing words		

- Work with your study partner and take it in turns to tell each other about a sport or hobby you enjoy doing. Make sure you give a number of important pieces of information followed by a supporting point or two. Try to end with an interesting point. Remember to maintain eye contact with your partner as you speak.

- When your partner has finished, complete the table below together.

Your partner

	Main information	Additional information
Sport		
Tough things		
Good things		
Closing words		

Part 1	The interview	
Part 2	**Individual long turn**	**3–4 mins**
Part 3	Two-way discussion	

Speaking

UNIT 3 Part two of the Speaking test – the long turn

In Part 2 of the test you will be asked to speak uninterrupted for up to two minutes, on a topic given to you by the examiner. The examiner will not talk during this time, but will be listening for the way in which your language flows, the appropriacy of the words you use, your grammatical accuracy and your pronunciation. Remember! The long turn is *your turn*, so make the most of it.

General points to remember!

- You will have a minute to think about what you are going to say and to make some notes.

- The topic will be general but you will be able to relate it to your own experience.

- The examiner will tell you your topic, but it will also be written in detail on a card. Read it carefully.

- Here is an example of a Part 2 task.

> Describe a zoo or a wildlife park you have visited that has impressed you.
>
> You should say:
>
> ◆ where it is situated
> ◆ when you went there
> ◆ how you felt about it

TEST TIP

Don't waste your minute. Use your minute's preparation wisely – make sure you write something down.
Don't try writing out the whole talk.
Don't stray from the topic.

PREPARING YOUR TALK

- Read the task carefully. Look for the key words in the first line. Decide quickly which zoo or wildlife park you are going to talk about.

- Note down some key words, using the sample below as a model. Include words which are specific to this topic.

- Make sure you mention something about each of the three additional points on the card.

- Try to give your talk some shape by making one to two main points – something that your listener might find interesting or want to know.

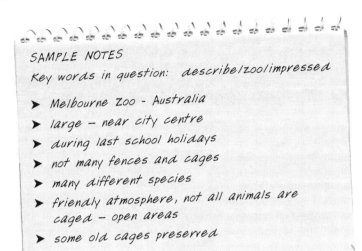

SAMPLE NOTES

Key words in question: describe/zoo/impressed

➤ Melbourne Zoo - Australia
➤ large – near city centre
➤ during last school holidays
➤ not many fences and cages
➤ many different species
➤ friendly atmosphere, not all animals are caged – open areas
➤ some old cages preserved

EXTRACT 1

- Listen to the first example of a long turn in Speaking Unit 3 Extract 1, based on the sample notes above.

- As you listen, have the speaker's notes in front of you and tick off the points that she makes in her talk. Then answer these questions.

1 Did she mention all the points in her notes?
2 Did she include anything new?
3 Which tense is used most?
4 Why is this tense used?
5 What, did you feel, is the speaker's main point?

CHECKING YOUR NOTES

- Give your notes about a visit to a zoo or wildlife park to your study partner. Use this checklist to decide how well his or her notes prepare for the long turn.

- Compare your notes with your partner's.

Checklist for notes	✔ ✗
Has he/she noted the key words from the question?	
Are there enough words to provide an idea of the shape and content of the talk?	
Has he/she addressed each point on the card?	
Are there any words which express feelings?	
Are there any words specifically related to the topic?	
Can you improve the notes in any way?	
How do you think he/she should end the talk?	

GIVING YOUR TALK

- Now take it in turns to give your talk to each other. Make sure that you speak for *one to two minutes*. Time yourselves, using a watch with a second hand.

- While your partner is talking, make some notes to form the basis of questions, which you can ask at the end of the talk.

- Try to give some constructive feedback to your partner and possibly some advice on how he or she could improve the talk.

- Record your talks, if you can, and play them back. Make a note of any areas which caused you difficulty, e.g. vocabulary, verb forms, tense, articles, pronunciation, ideas.

Follow-up activity 1

- Look at these expressions which the first speaker used. Try to find another way of expressing the same ideas.

I'm not that keen on … normally   e.g. I don't usually like …

It's really worth a visit.

They were very impressed …

From all over the world.

The zoo prides itself on

One interesting thing is that …

Follow-up activity 2

- Look at the expression 'One interesting thing is that …'. By changing the adjective, you can create similar expressions to introduce other ideas, e.g. *One unusual thing is that …*

- How many other expressions can you create, using this structure as your model?

Follow-up activity 3

EXTRACT 2

- Listen to the second example of a long turn about a visit to an African wildlife park, and note down the speaker's key words.

- Listen again and make a note of which adjectives he uses to describe how he felt at the time.

- Try to create the notes that the speaker might have made before he gave his talk.

- Listen a third time and write down any expressions that might be useful to you in your talk.

- Now answer these questions.

6 Which tense is used most?

7 Why is this tense used?

8 What, did you feel, was the speaker's main point?

Speaking

Part 1	The interview	
Part 2	**Individual long turn**	**3–4 mins**
Part 3	Two-way discussion	

UNIT 4 More practice for Part two

General points to remember

- There are four basic areas of proficiency which the examiner is listening for.
- You will be rated on the IELTS scale in each of these areas.
- They are all equally important.

Pre-speaking task

- Look at the four interlocking circles and the list of speaking skills.
- Make sure you understand all the words. Look up any words you do not understand in a dictionary.
- Match each skill to the appropriate area.

a Using linking words

b Using appropriate words

c Correcting yourself

d Using articles correctly

e Using the right tense

f Emphasising words to convey particular meaning

g Getting the stress right on long words

h Being able to keep going

i Finding a way of saying something even when you don't know the right word

j Being able to join your ideas together

k Being able to use complex sentences

l Making your language sound natural

m Getting the word order right

n Speaking clearly

o Having a knowledge of technical words

p Choosing words that go well together

q Using idiomatic language

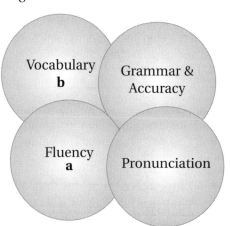

Vocabulary **b**

Grammar & Accuracy

Fluency **a**

Pronunciation

- What are you best at?
- What do you find most difficult about speaking English?
- What do you think are the most important skills for a good speaker to have?

TEST TIP

The long turn is not designed to test your general knowledge but to get you thinking and talking. So when you get your topic, don't be worried about what you don't know but rather, think of all the things you do know and draw on that knowledge.

118

BRAINSTORMING IDEAS

Brainstorming is a way of thinking of ideas quickly. You can do it as a class group or you can do it on your own.

- Spend about 10 minutes on this task. Look at the topics below. For each topic, see how many ideas come into your head – nouns, verbs, adjectives, proper nouns like places, people, etc. and write them down. Don't worry if some of them seem unusual. If they flow from the topic in some way for you, and you can explain that relationship, then they belong in your 'ideas bank'.

A medical advance that has benefited mankind

A person you have helped in your life

A river or a lake that you have visited

A future travel plan

A building that you particularly like

A film you have seen about a historical event

A job you would like to do in the future

A quiet place you enjoy visiting

A politician you admire

A book you read when you were at school

Your views on computer games

- Work through the topics in any order and try talking for one minute on the topic, using the ideas you thought of in the brainstorming exercise.
- Did you find any of these topics more interesting or appropriate for you than others? Why?

119

1 List the ways this Part 2 task is different from the previous task.

2 What effect will these differences have on the way you plan your talk?

> *Talk about a subject* you would like to study at some time in the future.*
>
> *You should say:*
> - *what the subject is*
> - *why you are interested in it*
> - *where you could possibly learn about it*
>
>   ** a hobby, a skill or an academic subject*

- Follow the points on page 115 of Unit 3 on how to prepare a talk.

- Make sure your notes contain key words and prompts for each of the different points of this topic.

- If working with another student, check each other's notes before you give your talks.

- Keep in mind the four areas on which you will be rated.

- Now give your talk and if possible, record it.

- Watch your timing carefully. Make sure you talk for *at least one minute* without stopping.

- Play the talk(s) back and listen carefully. Which of the four areas do you feel was your strongest area? Which was your weakest area?

- Play the talk(s) again and make some notes on your performance.

TEST TIP

After you have been speaking for about a minute, your examiner may signal that it is time to finish by asking you a follow-up question, such as 'Would you recommend this zoo to other people?' Answer this question briefly. It is not an invitation to continue your long turn.

	Things I did well	**Mistakes I made**
Fluency		
Vocabulary		
Grammatical Accuracy		Used wrong tense
Pronunciation	No intonation	

- How did you introduce your points?
- Was your talk interesting?

Part 1	*The interview*	
Part 2	*Individual long turn*	
Part 3	**Two-way discussion**	**4–5 mins**

Speaking

UNIT 5 Part three of the Speaking test – the two-way discussion

The two-way discussion is an opportunity to show your examiner that you can offer a reasoned point of view, appropriate to the question you have been asked. *The topic will be related to your long turn*, but will explore a more abstract side of the subject.

- In Unit 3 you practised talking about a zoo or wildlife park you had visited. Imagine that your examiner has now asked you this question.

> What do you think are the benefits of keeping animals in a zoo?

> I need to tell the examiner what I *think* are the good things about keeping animals in a zoo.

APPROACHING THE QUESTION

- Do you fully understand the question? Can you re-phrase the question (in your head) in your own words?

- Make a quick 'mental' list of one or two *benefits* or *negative points* about keeping animals in a zoo. Don't be afraid to say what you think. It's important to express opinions in the discussion.

- Decide whether any of the key words raise new questions. E.g. *A benefit to whom? What kind of zoo?* Could you refer to these in your response?

TEST TIP

Giving an opinion means having an opinion, but there is no right answer!

EXTRACT 1

- Listen to and read these possible responses. Which ones are the most appropriate? Why?
- Can you categorise them in any way? For example, similar opinions, similar style?
- Can you think of at least two other ways of answering the question?

a I believe there are a number of good reasons for keeping animals in a zoo. One is that you can see animals from other countries; animals you would never see in the wild. And zoos are really great for children, 'cos they can have the chance to see unusual animals.

b Personally, I don't like zoos. I can't see the point in them. You can see animals on the television, if that's what you want.

d I'm afraid I can't see any real benefits — at least not in the case of zoos. Though I may be wrong … Wildlife parks, on the other hand, are probably more useful, because they can actually help to protect animals from poachers or when there are environmental disasters such as drought.

c Well, I can see a number of benefits. Firstly they give us the chance to observe animal behaviour and they also help us protect certain species of animal, like the panda bear, for instance. Animals which may be under threat in the wild.

e I tend to think zoos can be of enormous benefit. But not just so that we can see rare and exotic beasts, or animals, but because they are … they act as a kind of research laboratory. But if I had my way, I'd probably keep the people out of the zoos – just keep them for the animals!

f There may be good things for us – humans. But I can't see what the poor animals get out of it. I mean, would you want to be stuck in a cage all day?

g I think the benefits of keeping animals in a zoo are that we can see animals such as lions and tigers, or kangaroos which you wouldn't normally see. Well, not where I come from, anyway. But some people think it's really cruel, and they may have a point.

WAYS TO BEGIN YOUR ANSWER

You can give an opinion without using an opening clause but it will sound very direct like the response f above. If you want to soften your response, it is better to start with an expression from the box below.

When you're sure or agree with the suggestion	**When you would like to put an alternative viewpoint**
I think / I don't think	I'm not sure …
I believe / I don't believe	I'm afraid I think …
Personally, I think / I don't think	Well, I don't know for sure but …
In my opinion / view	Possibly, but …
I can think of a couple of	I tend to think / believe

MORE PRACTICE ON THIS TOPIC

- Give well-reasoned responses to these further questions on the topic.
- Can you think of any more questions which the examiner could ask, based on this topic?

> You said that zoos in the past, used to be like prisons for the animals. But this has changed. What sort of changes have taken place in recent years to make zoos more humane?

> You mentioned that zoos are places where we can see wild animals. What do you think are the main differences between a so-called wild animal and a domesticated animal?

TEST TIP
The examiner will ask you questions on different aspects of the Part 2 topic, so the focus of the discussion will change with each new question.

ANTICIPATING THE ISSUES

- Turn back to page 119 in Unit 4 and look at the Part 2 topics again. Refer to your notes and 'ideas bank' from your earlier work, to remind yourself about these topics you practised for the long turn.
- Read the questions below and match them to the Part 2 topics.
- Write a question for each topic on page 119 for which there is no question below.

1 City life and rural life
People who live in cities often like to spend time in the countryside, to get away from the city. Why do you think this is so?

2 Books and young people
Why do many children seem to prefer playing computer games and watching sport to reading? What can we do to encourage young people to read more?

3 International aid
International organisations do invaluable work in areas where there is drought or famine. What is the best way to raise money to fund this sort of organisation?

4 The cinema
You mentioned you liked the cinema. But when a book is made into a film, sometimes the audiences are quite disappointed. Why do you think this is?

5 Health education
We hear a lot about advances in medicine, but do you think it might be better to spend money on ways of preventing illness, rather than on expensive medical treatment?

6 Architectural design
You said that the design of houses and buildings has changed in your country over the last 20 years. What do you think has driven these changes?

ASSESSING THE QUESTION

- As well as following the steps on page 121, it may help to consider what type of question it is. Does the examiner expect you to: give a reason, explain something, make an assessment, compare two things or look ahead?

- Work with your study partner for this activity.

- Go back to your 'ideas bank' for the topics from page 119.

- Work your way through the discussion questions above, taking it in turns to be the examiner and then the candidate.

- Try to give a fully rounded answer with a justification for your view in each case. The 'examiner' should think of at least one more question to ask each time after the 'candidate' has given his or her initial response.

- Try to establish a genuine dialogue on the topic. The 'candidate' should keep eye contact with the 'examiner' and talk confidently about their (his/her) ideas and opinions.

- If possible, record your answers. Listen to them using the checklist from Unit 4 to reflect on your performance.

TEST TIP

Remember this is a two-way discussion so be prepared to engage in the topic with your examiner.

Part 1	*The interview*	
Part 2	*Individual long turn*	
Part 3	***Two-way discussion***	***4–5 mins***

Speaking

UNIT 6 More practice for Part three

Part 3 of the test is designed to see how well you can carry on a discussion on a more abstract topic. The examiner will be listening out for your conversational strategies, as well as for accuracy, your use of vocabulary and your pronunciation.

WHAT'S THE QUESTION?

- Look at the responses below. Can you write a suitable Part 3 question for each one? You will need to work out what the topic is first.

- Look carefully at how each response begins and make sure your question fits both the meaning and the grammar. Try using both direct and indirect questions.

a

I don't think we should waste money on trying to build a kind of colony in space because, frankly, we have enough problems on Earth which we need to fix first.

b

Personally, I prefer modern museums, where you can actually do things, or see how something works. Old-fashioned museums seem pretty boring to me.

c

That's a hard question! But no! I think single sex schools are probably better. They say that girls do better at single sex schools, you know, but boys don't, apparently.

d

Well, we have to remember that you could be put in prison, when you're completely innocent, simply on the evidence of your fingerprints. So … no! I think DNA sampling … has to be better, surely.

e

Well, no, I don't think so, because I'm one of those people who likes relaxing on holiday, not climbing mountains! But, obviously, for some people, adventure holidays are really exciting.

USING ADVERBS TO EXPRESS AN OPINION

- We can use adverbs to make an argument stronger. For example, we can say *Clearly, there's been a mistake* instead of saying *It is clear that there's been a mistake.*

- Look at the responses on page 125. Find the adverbs used and make sure you understand them.

- Now rephrase these sentences using the adverb in brackets to make the point more forcefully.

- Now ask and answer the question you wrote to responses a–e. Use adverbs to highlight your meaning.

1 According to the telephone technician, we don't need another telephone line for our fax machine. (apparently)

2 To be absolutely frank, I think the idea of the monarchy is completely out of date. (frankly)

3 I am not in favour of sports like fox-hunting, or even horse-racing, but that's just my opinion. (personally)

4 There is evidence that the bushfires were started deliberately which is hard to believe, but true. (apparently/ regrettably)

5 Some people must enjoy horror movies because otherwise they wouldn't keep making them. (Obviously)

6 They say it's quite easy to book a flight on the Internet, but I've never had much luck with it myself. (theoretically)

7 Everyone travels by plane today. The days of the great passenger liners are gone, which is a shame in a way. (regrettably)

8 I'd like to think I could finish my degree in three years but I don't think it's really possible. (realistically)

9 The government spends thousands of dollars on anti-smoking campaigns, so we hope to see a change in people's smoking habits. (hopefully)

10 I'm surprised we have to buy another text book because they haven't changed the syllabus. (surely)

GIVING AN OPINION

TEST TIP

There will always be more than one way to answer the question.

- Turn back to Listening Unit 7 pages 26–27 and read the extracts. Try to identify the topic of each extract, e.g. science, language, etc.

- Match the questions on page 127 to the paragraphs on pages 26–27.

- Now respond to each question. Think about what language you can use to make your argument stronger. Remember that the examiner just wants to hear you give an opinion. There are no right answers and you will not be marked for this opinion.

i You're learning English at the moment. But how easy would it be for me to learn your language? For example, what aspects of your language make it particularly different from English?

Would you like to teach your language to people from other countries?

ii Some people say we are born the way we are and we can't change ourselves. Other people say we learn everything from our experiences and our environment. What do you think?

Do you think people are born naturally 'good at music' or 'good at maths'?

iii Understanding the physical world around us is fascinating for some people but others find it uninteresting. How important do you think it is to study physics at school?

What are the benefits of teaching subjects like biology and chemistry at school?

iv Every culture has its own myths and folk tales but these days they may seem boring or irrelevant. Do you think it is useful to maintain these aspects of our culture?

What is the best way to make sure that children grow up knowing about their cultural past?

Think again

- What did you find most difficult about these questions? E.g. lack of appropriate vocabulary, knowledge of the topic, etc.
- What aspects of the topics were easier? Why?

Frequently asked questions about the Speaking test

Q What do I do if I don't understand a word in the question?
A You can ask the examiner to explain the word.

Q What do I do if I can't think of anything to say?
A Start thinking quickly! You won't be asked a question on a different topic and if you change the topic, or produce a learned talk, you will definitely lose marks.

Q What does it mean if the examiner says "Thank you" to me?
A Finish what you are saying. It means that it is time to stop that part of the test.

Q What do I do if I realise, while I'm talking, that I haven't understood the question?
A Show that you may have misunderstood. Then the examiner can steer you back on target.

Q What do I do if the examiner interrupts me?
A Stop and listen.

Q Are the four speaking criteria rated equally?
A Yes, they are. So make sure you pay equal attention to them all.

Q Are the three parts of the speaking test rated equally?
A Yes, they are.

Recording Script

Words *in italics* indicate the location of answers to the listening exercises.

UNIT 1, EXTRACT 1

1

TOURIST	We're looking for the bus station. Can you tell us if it's round here?
WOMAN	Um, let me think. You go down to the traffic lights and then turn left. The bus station is on your right. You can't miss it.
TOURIST	Thanks very much.

2

CUSTOMER	I need a copy of a book called 'Statistics for First Year Students' by MJ Hawthorn. Do you have it in stock?
ASSISTANT	You're the third person who's asked for that today – I'm afraid there's been a bit of a run on that book and we're out of stock at the moment. We do have it on order though, and it should be coming in at the end of the week.
CUSTOMER	Oh! Well, can you keep a copy for me?
ASSISTANT	Certainly. Can I have your name?

3

TEACHER	Good morning, Chris!
STUDENT	Morning, Mr Simons!
TEACHER	Running a bit late, aren't you? The bell's already gone!
STUDENT	Bus was late, sir!

4

STUDENT	Excuse me. I'm looking for the Medical school. Do you know if I'm going in the right direction?
WOMAN	Sure, um. Go along this road, here, past the library and past the Great Hall. The Faculty of Medicine is on your left. It's about three minutes' walk from here.
STUDENT	Thanks very much.

5

BOY 1	I've got this really cool new computer game – it's called Soccer Superstars.
BOY 2	How does it work? Can I have a look?
BOY 1	Sure. Well first you choose your own club – you know, Inter Milan, Manchester United…
BOY 2	Right!
BOY 1	And then you actually manage the team as if you were the club manager. It's all about tactics.
BOY 2	Cool!

6

WOMAN	Welcome to the Millennium School of English. We're delighted that you've chosen to come and study with us here in Boston and we hope you'll be very happy and enjoy your stay. Now… I'd like to start by introducing you to our team of highly experienced teachers. Our head…

7

STUDENT	Oh Hi! I'd really like to be able to play for one of the university football teams. How do you…like…become a member of the club?
COACH	Well to join one of the university teams, you'll have to demonstrate that you're already a good player.
STUDENT	Right! Fair enough.
COACH	We're having trials down here on the oval next Tuesday at 6 o'clock. So if you come along, we'll have a look at you then.
STUDENT	OK – I'll, I'll do that.

8

NEWSREADER	Newcastle express derailed outside the station. Presidential elections cause a riot in Florida and petrol prices set to rise again. This is the six o'clock news – and I'm Sally Broadmoore. Good evening!

9

MALE	I'm standing outside the Sydney Football Ground, crowds are pouring in for tonight's international match between Australia and New Zealand, and the atmosphere here is absolutely electric. This is going to be a fantastic match. So let's go over to the changing rooms and have a word with the New Zealand captain.

10

CUSTOMER	I'm interested in buying a laptop computer. Can you give me some information about these two here?
ASSISTANT	Sure! Right. What sort of price range were you looking at?
CUSTOMER	Oh, not sure really.
ASSISTANT	OK… well this one has a built in DVD as well as modem so it's pretty versatile. It weighs under 2 kgs, which is quite an advantage. It's our most popular model – at £1495 it's pretty good value.
CUSTOMER	Right – Yes, I need to be able to carry it around easily. Does it have a clear screen…

UNIT 1, EXTRACT 2

INTERVIEWER	Good morning! We're doing a brief survey on student use of the food outlets at the university. Would you mind answering a few questions?
STUDENT 1	OK. But make it brief.
INTERVIEWER	Sure! It won't take long. Which of the three

UNIT 2, EXTRACT 5

WOMAN 1	University. Good morning.
MAN 1	Oh, good morning. Can you put me through to the School of Architecture, please?
WOMAN 1	Certainly.
WOMAN 2	School of Architecture. Professor Dawson's office.
MAN 1	Oh! Good morning. I was wondering if you could give me some information about the forthcoming Architecture 21 conference? Dates, enrolment procedures, costs…that sort of thing?
WOMAN 2	Certainly.
MAN 1	When exactly is the conference?
WOMAN 2	Well, the conference runs for three days from the *18th to the 20th of October*.
MAN 1	*18th–20th October*…oh good. I'll still be here then and um… where exactly is it being held? Is it at the university as in previous years?
WOMAN 2	No, it's actually being held at the *Pacific Hotel –* we've rather outgrown the university conference facilities so we've opted for this new venue.
MAN 1	Right – Paradise Hotel.
WOMAN 2	No … *Pacific Hotel*.
MAN 1	Oh, right. And presumably we can get accommodation at the hotel?
WOMAN 2	Yes, but you'll need to contact them direct to arrange that. I'll give you the number for hotel reservations. Have you got a pen ready?
MAN 1	Yeah, go ahead.
WOMAN 2	It's area code *(07) and then 9 triple three double two double three.*
MAN 1	*07 9, triple three double 2 double 3.* And what's the registration fee?
WOMAN 2	Individual fees are $300 for the 3 days, or $120 a day if you only wanted to attend for one day.
MAN 1	Are there any student concessions?
WOMAN 2	Oh, sure. There's a 50% concession for students, and that's $150 for the three days, or *$60 a day*.
MAN 1	And am I too late to offer to give a talk?
WOMAN 2	Oh, I'm pretty sure you've missed the deadline for that.
MAN 1	Oh, really! But I've only just arrived here in Australia – is there any way I could have a paper accepted?
WOMAN 2	Well, you'd need to *talk to Professor Dawson*. He's the person organising the conference this year. I can put you through, if you like?
MAN 1	Oh, yes please. That'd be great. Oh and can I just check the spelling of his name? Is that DAWSON?
WOMAN 2	Yes, that's correct.

DAWSON	Professor Dawson speaking.
HELSTONE	Oh, hello. My name's John Helstone. I'm an architecture student at London University. I'm here in Australia for 3 months, looking at energy saving house designs.
DAWSON	Right.
HELSTONE	I'm interested in giving a talk on my research at the conference but I believe I may have missed the deadline.
DAWSON	Well, strictly speaking you have. *The closing date was last Friday*.
HELSTONE	Oh, no!
DAWSON	But we may be able to include your paper if it fits into our program… but you'll have to be quick.
HELSTONE	OK. What do I need to do?
DAWSON	Send me an outline of your talk. And make sure you include *an interesting title for the talk*. Something to attract the delegates' attention.
HELSTONE	OK. Interesting title. Right.
DAWSON	The outline should be *no more than 300 words, though*.
HELSTONE	Right. I should be able to keep it down to 300 words but would 400 be OK?
DAWSON	No, not really because we have to print it in the proceedings and we just don't have the space.
HELSTONE	Sure! I understand.
DAWSON	And also, can you send me *a short CV –* the usual stuff, name, age, qualifications. That sort of thing.
HELSTONE	Right. *Include a brief CV*.
DAWSON	Actually, you can e-mail it to me. That'd be quicker.
HELSTONE	Sure. What's your e-mail address?
DAWSON	Well the best thing would be to send it to the conference administrative officer. The address is *admin – in lower case. You know, in small letters*.
HELSTONE	Right.
DAWSON	So that's A D M I N at uniconf dot E D U dot A U.
HELSTONE	Right. I'll do that straight away. Thank you very much. You've been very helpful.
DAWSON	OK. Well, we hope to see you in October, then.

UNIT 3 EXTRACT 1

Mini-talk 1

MAN

We believe there was a game, similar to football, played in Japan as well as in China as far back as 1000 BC. But unfortunately, very little is known about this. The Romans apparently played a game which sort of resembled modern soccer, but they had 27 men to a team! Can you imagine that? Modern soccer dates from the 19th century and has its origins in England. These days the game is played by women as well as men.

Mini-talk 2

MAN

I think the most famous player ever would have to be the Brazilian, Pelé. In his time, he was the most well paid and possibly the most famous athlete in the world. He led his national team, the Brazilian team, to win no fewer than three World Cups in 1958, in 1962 and then again in 1970.

In November 1969 he scored his 1,000th goal. Pelé also won an International Peace Award in 1978 and became a national hero.

Mini-talk 3

MAN

As far as we know, the earliest known rules for what we call 'modern' soccer are believed to have been created in 1815 at a famous boys' school in England called Eton College, where the game used to be played. Before this date, there weren't really any rules as such! The rules are now very complex and are constantly under review. From time to time FIFA, that's the international body governing the game, FIFA makes changes to the rules. Referees come under enormous pressure both from the crowds and the players, but it's against the rules to argue with the ref!

Mini-talk 4

MAN

The first World Cup was organised in 1930 by FIFA, the international body governing the game, and this competition was won by Uruguay. The World Cup is played every four years and the competition consists of a number of tournaments being played around the world, leading to an elimination event with 16 teams from 16 different countries. The last World Cup attracted TV audiences of approximately 35 billion people for almost 27 days. This makes soccer *the* most watched sport in the history of the world.

Mini-talk 5

MAN

The first league was formed in England in 1888. Twelve of the strongest clubs at the time formed the league and played in competition against one another. In 1892 a second division was formed and soon after this the league adopted the practice, at the end of the season, of promoting the first two clubs in the second division to the first division and the last two clubs in the first division were sent down to the second division. Other countries soon followed suit and formed their own leagues.

UNIT 3, EXTRACT 2

ANNOUNCER

Jon Getnick is with us in the studio tonight to talk about the origins of the game of chess. Welcome Jon.

GETNICK

Thank you. I'm sure you are all familiar with the wonderful game of chess. But have you ever stopped to think about where it came from and when? Well, we think chess has its origins either in Afghanistan or *in what is now northern India* and dates from some time before 600AD. That's nearly fifteen hundred years ago. The oldest written references that we have to chess date from then, but there are unverified claims that chess existed as early as 100 AD *so the game could, in fact, go back 2000 years*. Let's look first at the rules. *The rules of standard chess are firmly fixed and internationally agreed upon*, but there are some variations

to the rules found in various parts of the world. For instance, one variation of chess is called Shogi and is played in Japan. *Another variation is played in China.*

We think the version played by Europeans and Americans today travelled through Iran, to the main commercial centres of Italy and Spain and we are pretty certain that it was there by about 1000 AD. The game was then taken into Scandinavia by the sea-faring Vikings and it was well *established in Central Europe by 1400 AD* and by then the rules which we use today were in place.

The modern *chess pieces date from the 1800s* and are known as Staunton pieces. Staunton was an English chess master in the mid 1800s and it's his design which is used in tournaments all over the world.

But tournaments are a reasonably recent phenomenon. The first official chess tournament was played in 1866 in London. On this occasion, to restrict the length of the game and limit the time spent on each move, they used a particular type of clock *known as a 'sand clock'*.

Let's have a look, now, at some of the big names in the history of the game. The 1866 London tournament was won by a man from Bohemia by the name of Steinitz. This man was, in effect, *the world's first official champion* and he held the title until 1894 when he was beaten by a man living in America called Emanuel Lasker, who had been born in Germany. Lasker remained the champ until 1921 when the title was taken off him by a Cuban called Capablanca. Many people today consider Capablanca as one of *the top three players* ever to live. Another player in this category is Bobby Fischer, who became the US champion at the age of only 14 and was *the first native-born US citizen, actually born in America* to have held the title of World Chess Champion.

UNIT 4, EXTRACT 1

Dialogue 1

WOMAN Do you need some help or are you happy just browsing?

MAN I'm okay, thanks.

WOMAN Just let me know if you want *to try anything on*. We've got more sizes out the back in case you can't find your size on the racks.

MAN Thanks, I'm fine.

WOMAN Right you are!

Dialogue 2

MAN *I'm after* a book by Patrick White. It doesn't seem to be anywhere on the shelves.

WOMAN Which 'Patrick White' *are you after?*

MAN I think it's called *The Tree of Life.*

WOMAN No. It's called *The Tree of Man*, actually.

MAN Yes, that's it. Sorry! It's on the reading list for First Year Australian literature…

WOMAN Yes, well it's out, I'm afraid. We hold four copies of that title, but they're all out at the moment. Would you like to reserve it for next week?

MAN No thanks. I'll have to buy a copy. I'm supposed to have it read by Monday!

Dialogue 3

WOMAN 1 Do you have the university T-shirt in a size 12 in blue?

WOMAN 2 We may have. But everything we've got is on the racks over there.

WOMAN 1 Oh, okay. So you haven't got a size 12, by the looks of it?

WOMAN 2 Not if there isn't one there. We've got it in the pink, I believe.

WOMAN 1 Uh! No thanks. I'm not really a 'pink' person.

WOMAN 2 *Sorry, love! We're out of the blue.*

Dialogue 4

WOMAN 1 Good morning. Can I help you?

WOMAN 2 Good morning. Do you have a copy of George Orwell's 'Animal Farm'? It's a set text for an exam I'm preparing for.

WOMAN 1 We do normally keep that one. Let me just *look it up* on the computer. Yes, according to this we have three copies in stock.

WOMAN 1 How much is it?

WOMAN 2 It's 15.95. It's over there – in the Modern Classics section.

WOMAN 1 Thanks. And also, *I'm looking for* a good book on English verbs. Can you recommend anything?

WOMAN 2 Well, rather than my recommending something, why don't you go and have a look in our very comprehensive grammar and reference section? I'm sure you'll find something.

WOMAN 1 Thanks.

Dialogue 5

WOMAN Morning! Student Medical Centre.

MAN Can I make an appointment to see one of the doctors today, please?

WOMAN I can give you 2 o'clock tomorrow afternoon or 9am on Friday.

MAN Nothing earlier? I'm feeling really terrible and I'm sure I'm running a temperature.

WOMAN Sorry! The doctors are all fully *booked up* today. If you need emergency treatment, I suggest you go to the hospital.

MAN Thanks.

Dialogue 6

MAN Oh, good evening. I'd like to see one of the doctors, please.

NURSE Sure. Take a seat and I'll be right with you.

MAN Thanks.

NURSE Now, before you can see the doctor, I need you *to fill out* this form so that we can get your details. Have you been to this Casualty Department before?

MAN Uh… no! I don't think so.

NURSE Can I have your name?

Dialogue 7

WOMAN Can I come in?

MAN Sure – come in. Oh hi, Mariella. How's it going?

WOMAN Oh, okay! But I've *run into* a bit of a problem with my Economics essay topic.

MAN Right! What's the problem?

WOMAN Well, initially I wanted to do something on the slump in the Internet industry, but I just haven't been able to *get hold of* enough data and so I was wondering if you'd be prepared to give me an extension until Wednesday week to get my essay in.

MAN Well…. As long as you promise…

Dialogue 8

STUDENT 2 Hello?

STUDENT 1 Hi, Frank! It's Greg here.

STUDENT 2 How ya going?

STUDENT 1 Good, mate. Doing anything this evening?

STUDENT 2 Yes! I've got to finish my Economics essay. Why?

STUDENT 1 Oh! It's just that there's a free barbecue on at the Sports Centre – thought you might fancy coming along?

STUDENT 2 Look , I'd love to, but if I don't finish my essay for Dr Pollard tonight I may as well *give up* Economics. In fact, I may as well *give up* university! I only just scraped a pass in first semester!

STUDENT 1 Oh well. Don't let me keep you from your books.

STUDENT 2 Thanks. Have fun, anyway.

Dialogue 9

STUDENT 1 Sandra! Are you going to play any sport this season, by that I mean, play for one of the university teams?

STUDENT 2 No. I don't think so. I played basketball last year for the uni. It was fun but it really *cut into* my time. This year I thought I'd focus on my studies a bit.

STUDENT 1 Really? I'm thinking of *signing up* for the rowing club, but you have to be prepared to train three mornings a week at 5 o'clock, plus you have to *give up* all your Saturdays for the competitions.

STUDENT 2 Oh, well! Good luck with it.

Dialogue 10

CLERK Next, please!

STUDENT Good morning. Yes! I'd like to *pay off* my overdraft, please. I think I owe about $50.00.

CLERK Right. Do you have your account here at this branch?

STUDENT Yes, I do.

CLERK What's your account number?

STUDENT Um… I think it's this one here.

CLERK Yes. That looks right. How would you like to settle that?

STUDENT With cash…

UNIT 4, EXTRACT 2

ANNOUNCER

Paddling around on a river in a small boat is not everyone's idea of fun. Canoes, which are narrow boats to start with and usually hold one or two people at the most, are particularly well-known for being unstable and turning over in the water. But more and *more people are taking boats like this out* onto dangerous rivers to enjoy what is called 'white-water canoeing'. Cynthia Barton, one of Britain's top canoeists talks about what the sport is and how to get started if you're thinking of taking it up.

CYNTHIA

A lot of people may be familiar with what I call recreational canoeing. That's where you take a canoe out onto a nice calm river, with a picnic and have a very relaxing time. But if you're doing white-water canoeing then you're doing something very different. For a start, *you have to do it on a fast-flowing river.* You've got to be moving quickly through the water and when you're doing that, you make a lot of froth and bubbles and the water looks white. That's basically where the name comes from. Also, unlike recreational canoeing, white-water canoeing is a competitive sport. It involves racing on a river against other canoeists to see who can win… and there are two main ways that this is done.

The first is the typical race to see who can *follow a straight line*, between two points on the river, in the quickest time. Just like a runner on a race track. The second, and more challenging type of race, is one in which the participants have to steer their canoe *in and out of poles* along the river in order to reach the end of the race…*more like a skier.*

So where do you go to do it? Well, although you can canoe on most rivers, those that are ideal for white-water canoeing are hard to come by and enthusiastic canoeists regularly travel quite long distances to find the right water. If you're prepared to go there, *Scotland has numerous popular rivers like the Tay and Tweed, and Wales is also very good for white-water canoeing.* And on the other side of the world, I believe the sport is catching on in parts of Australia and New Zealand too.

Of course, you've also got to think about equipment. You need to get yourself a good canoe and these can set you back anything from *£300 to £700* depending on the material they're made of. The more you can pay, the better really. Personally, I wouldn't look at anything under £500, but that obviously depends on your budget. You also need a hard helmet to protect yourself against rocks when you fall out of the canoe – and believe me you will fall out. Because of this, there's no point, particularly as a beginner, *in wearing anything but a wet suit.* That's a must.

I think it's worth saying that once you *get* started, the important thing is not to be put off the sport early on, by allowing someone to tempt you to canoe on a river that's just too difficult. The popular rivers are, in fact, graded from 1 to 6 in the same way that ski runs are graded to tell people just how flat or steep they are. The higher the grade, the more difficult the river is, *so a grade 1 river which is basically no different from a canal, is the best one to start with.* Once you're an expert, which can take some time, you can, of course, try anything…and really serious canoeists, who want a real challenge, go out a lot more in the winter when the water level is high and *deliberately look for the most dangerous rivers.*

Whatever you say about this sport, it is never dull. Generally it's a fantastic sport for anyone who likes adventure. On another level it's a serious activity and you can become a real champion but it's a small group who take it that far.

UNIT 5, EXTRACT 1

Example

MAN   What did you think of the movie 'The Lord of the Rings'?

WOMAN   I really enjoyed it. And I thought the music was great.

MAN   Yes, I thought so too.

Conversation 1

WOMAN   What age do you think people should be able to get married at?

MAN   Oh, I dunno! Eighteen, I suppose. Sixteen seems very young.

WOMAN   Yes, I think so too. But in most countries, the legal age for getting married is, in fact, 16.

MAN   In my opinion, that's just too young, isn't it? I mean, you can't even vote at 16.

Conversation 2

WOMAN   What subjects are you studying this year?

MAN   I'm doing Accounting and Statistics as part of a Commerce degree. But I'm finding it pretty dull, to tell you the truth.

WOMAN   Yes, I feel very much the same about Statistics. But it'll get better next year.

Conversation 3

MAN 1   I've been reading about the International Space Station that they're building in space. You know, I'd love to spend some time up there.

MAN 2   I can't think of anything worse. And space travel isn't at all good for the body, you know. It draws the calcium out of your bones.

MAN 1   Maybe not, but I find this stuff absolutely fascinating. The Space Station is a truly international venture. I'd go tomorrow!

Conversation 4

WOMAN   Did you know that we waste hundreds of litres of water every day, simply because people don't turn off their taps properly?

MAN   The problem is, that people can't see that by turning off their tap, or switching off a light in their house, they are saving litres of water and hundreds of trees.

WOMAN   I know. That's right.

Conversation 5

MAN I don't think teenagers should be forced to stay at school if they really aren't enjoying it.

WOMAN 1 Oh, I'm not so sure about that. I don't think they really know what's good for them. How can they?

WOMAN 2 Yes, but the problem is probably with the education system rather than the kids themselves. School can be incredibly boring!

Conversation 6

MAN I've just been to the new Tate art gallery in London. I thought it was great.

WOMAN 1 Did you? Frankly, I don't like it very much myself. I prefer the old Tate.

MAN Oh, really? I think it shows an interesting use of space.

WOMAN 2 But that's the fashion these days, isn't it? Museums and art galleries all around the world are being housed in old warehouses and power stations. I think it's quite a good idea, really, the concept of recycling buildings!

Conversation 7

WOMAN I'm voting for the Opposition party on Saturday. I'm fed up with the present government.

MAN 1 I haven't quite decided who to vote for, but you know the old saying 'Better the devil you know…'

MAN 2 Oh, I agree with Sarah. I think we need a change.

Conversation 8

MAN I'm doing a survey on shopping habits. Would you mind answering a couple of quick questions?

WOMAN OK. As long as it doesn't take long.

MAN How often do you eat hamburgers?

WOMAN Never. I'm a vegetarian. I don't eat any animal products.

MAN Right! Can I just ask you? Are you wearing leather shoes?

WOMAN Yes, I am.

MAN Don't you think that's rather hypocritical?

WOMAN No, not really.

MAN I would have thought it was, myself!

Conversation 9

WOMAN Look at this. Sport on the front page of the newspapers again. It's ridiculous. Who cares which team won on Saturday?

MAN 1 Oh, come on, Laura. Just because you're not interested in football…

WOMAN That's not the point. I just think that as a society, we spend far too much time talking about sport and not nearly enough time worrying about real issues.

MAN 2 I think Susan's got a point. Sport's a substitute for things that matter…a way of distracting us.

Conversation 10

WOMAN What *is* that music you're listening to?

MAN It's Miles Davis…Don't you like jazz?

WOMAN No. It gives me a headache. I don't know what you see in it. Can't you play some decent music for a change, Mozart or Beethoven?

MAN Sorry, I don't have any classical music!

UNIT 5, EXTRACT 2

Introduction A

WOMAN Good morning!

MAN Hi.

WOMAN Can I help you? Are you looking for anything in particular?

MAN Yes, I'm trying to get hold of a book called um…It's a set text for First Year Economics…I'm afraid I can't remember the exact title but it's by somebody called Barnaby, I think.

WOMAN Oh yes. I know it. It's by Barnabus and Bailey.

Introduction B

INTERVIEWER Welcome to this week's edition of 'The Sports Show'. Today, we're going to look at the role of the sports coach in elite sport. In the studio we have a group of young athletes and two coaches from two very different sports, football and gymnastics. And let's go first to Charlie McPhee who's been coaching young footballers for over 25 years. Charlie, welcome to the programme.

McPHEE My pleasure!

Introduction C

MAN OK, everyone! Let's get started. We've got three tutorial papers to get through in the next hour so… who's going first?

WOMAN 1 We are, Dr. Matthews! Cathy and I are doing a joint presentation this week.

MAN Oh yes. Of course! And can you just remind the rest of the group what area of the media you've chosen to research?

WOMAN 2 Yes, well. We've been looking at the effect of television on young children.

MAN Right. Over to you.

Introduction D

TUTOR Good morning, everyone. I'd like to introduce our guest to you, John Watson. We're delighted to have John with us today to share his views on conservation. As Environmental Science students, I know you'll have a lot of questions, so let's kick off by asking him to tell us how he got involved in the environmental movement.

WATSON Thank you, Deborah. It's nice to be here…

Introduction E

INTERVIEWER Welcome to this week's addition of 'Frontiers of Science'. The International Space Station – the ISS – is a floating laboratory, 350 km above the Earth. But what exactly is it and who is behind it? To answer our questions, we are pleased to welcome to the studio, Dr Karl Richter who is a specialist in the field of space research.

RICHTER Delighted to be here.

UNIT 5, EXTRACT 3

TUTOR Good morning, everyone. I'd like to introduce our guest to you, John Watson. We're delighted to have John with us today to share his views on conservation. As Environmental Science students, I know you'll have a lot of questions, so let's kick off by asking him to tell us how he got involved in the environmental movement.

WATSON Thank you, Deborah. It's nice to be here. When I was seven years old, back in the 1940s, my father bought 200 acres of land on the Central Coast of New South Wales in eastern Australia. The marvellous thing about it was that it was *virgin bush*, in other words, *completely natural*. But this kind of country doesn't exist any more.

TUTOR What do you mean by that?

WATSON Well…let me explain. We went to live there when I was 10. When I was 12, the foxes and cats appeared. And by the time I was 14, there were no native animals left.

STUDENT 1 You mean, that *within 4 years, all the native animals had gone?*

WATSON That's exactly what I mean. But it took a while for people to realise what was going on.

STUDENT 2 So you're saying that it was *the cat and the fox that killed off the native animals?*

WATSON Absolutely right! But back in the 1970s people didn't realise it. Even though Australia was losing wildlife faster than the rest of the world combined, *people were blaming the farmers and miners*, but not their lovely little pussy cats!

TUTOR Their domestic cats, you're talking about?

WATSON Exactly. And what's more, they didn't want to know!

TUTOR Can you tell us how you set about proving your theory that it was feral cats and foxes which were killing native animals?

WATSON Well, I moved to South Australia specifically to set up a wildlife sanctuary there.

TUTOR Why South Australia in particular?

WATSON I chose South Australia because it was the only state where it was still legal for me to fence off an area and put back locally extinct animals.

STUDENT 1 That was very far sighted of them, wasn't it?

WATSON Well, not exactly. *They just hadn't got around to making it illegal!* Though they soon tried to, once they realised what I was doing.

STUDENT 1 Did you ever get into trouble for your actions?

WATSON Yes. Once or twice! In 1976 they put me in jail *for cutting down some pine trees to allow me to build a fence, to keep out the cats and foxes.*

TUTOR How did you get out of that situation?

WATSON Oh, well. I signed an agreement, saying that I wouldn't go on building the sanctuary, but then I just kept on building it!

STUDENT 1 That was very brave of you!

WATSON Well, *I figured that I had signed under duress, so I didn't feel bound by it.* The sanctuary was completed in 1983 and opened to the public in 1985. And within a year, it was overrun with native animals.

STUDENT 1 There are other ways of protecting endangered animals, though, aren't there? You can raise public awareness *through research and educational programs.*

WATSON Well, I don't have much time for that. Unfortunately, today we measure success in science not by your results but by how much funding you get.

STUDENT 2 What you've done is obviously admirable. But don't you think there's an argument for letting nature take its course? *I mean, don't you think cats and foxes have a right to live too?*

WATSON Well, no. Not really. They were introduced to this country but they don't belong here.

STUDENT 2 But aren't you trying to turn back the clock? *These other animals are here now.* What is so important to you about native species that justifies killing any number of alien ones?

WATSON I believe that evolution gave us a paradise and that we will lose everything unless we understand the need for balance. *But really, at the end of the day, it's just a belief, it's just a feeling…*

UNIT 6, EXTRACT 1

A

WOMAN Even though I told her not to bother, my friend insisted on driving me to the airport.

B

WOMAN On top of everything else, we now have to worry about my sick grandmother, too.

C

MAN Finally, before we go, I'd just like to thank you all for coming along to the meeting this evening.

D

WOMAN No matter what you do, you can't avoid growing older each year, but for your own sake, you can at least try to stay fit.

E

MAN   As a result of the burglary, we have decided to put bars on the windows.

F

WOMAN   Not only is the new law going to make it more expensive to smoke cigarettes, it's also going to discourage young people from taking it up in the first place – which has to be a good thing.

G

MAN   People always think that foreign languages are spoken much faster than their own language. For example, they say: 'Don't New Yorkers speak fast!' but in reality, it's just a problem of understanding.

UNIT 6, EXTRACT 2

INTERVIEWER   Welcome to this week's edition of 'Frontiers of Science'. The International Space Station – the ISS – is a floating laboratory, 350 km above the Earth. But what exactly is it and who is behind it? To answer our questions, we are pleased to welcome to the studio, Dr Karl Richter who is a specialist in the field of space research.

RICHTER   Delighted to be here.

INTERVIEWER   Dr. Richter! Who is behind this venture?

RICHTER   The International Space Station, the ISS, is a joint venture between America, Russia, Japan, Canada, Brazil and the 15 nations of the European Space Agency.

INTERVIEWER   So that's … 18,19 *twenty countries in all.*

RICHTER   Yes, that's correct. **And on top of that**, it's the largest and most complex international scientific project in history.

INTERVIEWER   Wow! And can you tell us how much it's going to cost?

RICHTER   Well, *despite the fact that it was estimated to cost 120 billion dollars*, it has already gone 8 billion over budget, so now we're looking at 128 billion.

INTERVIEWER   And what size will it be?

RICHTER   Well … it will measure 108m across by 88m long with almost half a hectare of solar panels powering six scientific laboratories.

INTERVIEWER   OK. So it's no small venture, is it? Now, I must ask you this question. What do they do about water on board?

RICHTER   Good question! Well, *nothing goes to waste.* But, hygiene in space is a complex affair! **Because of** the impracticality of transporting large amounts of liquid into space, they've come up with some ingenious solutions. **For instance**, everything on board, including the laboratory rats, loses water when it exhales or sweats. The humidity goes through a condensation *process before being returned to the water supply.*

INTERVIEWER   I see.

RICHTER   *If they didn't re-use the water*, the station would need about 20,000kg of water a year, which just couldn't be done.

INTERVIEWER   Going back to the laboratories. What's going to be happening there?

RICHTER   Well, we'll have teams of astronaut-scientists working in the labs and research will include, **for example** tissue culture, *studying life in low gravity*, the nature of space, observations of the Earth from space with a view to improving our maps, and the development of new commercial products.

INTERVIEWER   I can't imagine what it must be like to live without gravity, though we've probably all seen those pictures of people trying to eat and drink in *a state of weightlessness.*

RICHTER   Indeed. And of course, **in addition to this**, we don't really know what the long term mental *effects on the human psyche* will be. So that is a particular area of interest.

INTERVIEWER   Can you give us an idea of what life is like on board. What's the daily routine for the astronauts?

RICHTER   Well, you need to be real good friends with the others because it's a small place! The first chore of the day each morning is to ensure all is well with the many systems. **Then** this is followed by breakfast which is timed to take precisely 45 minutes. Experts have decided that togetherness around the dining table is psychologically important, so meals of pre-packed food are eaten together.

INTERVIEWER   Is that right?

RICHTER   Mail received overnight is read around the breakfast table, *followed by a daily conference. So meetings are inescapable*, even in space!

INTERVIEWER   And what about recreational time?

RICHTER   It's pretty brief and facilities are minimal. **But for instance**, some astronauts prefer to read, others listen to CDs. One guy, I understand, just used to stare out of the window. *Each day*, **in order to** offset the ill effects of being cooped up in the astronauts' environment, they have *two hours set aside for exercise*. Work rosters occupy six 12-hour days each week. Sundays are for rest and communication, via e-mails and video conferencing with family back home on Earth.

INTERVIEWER   So how is the schedule progressing? Is the project on time?

RICHTER   So so. **The first two components** which are

known as the 'Unity' module and 'the Zarya' module, were launched in 1998 and were then *joined together. Joining them together took 12 days.*

INTERVIEWER   Incredible! I don't know how they do that stuff!

RICHTER   **And the next stage** took place in May 1999, when the space shuttle 'Discovery' and its crew delivered two tonnes of equipment. This has been stored, awaiting the arrival of the first crew.

INTERVIEWER   OK. And how do the astronauts actually survive?

RICHTER   There's a Russian supply module which was attached in July 2000. *It provides air, water and food for the astronauts,* as well as electricity for experiments.

INTERVIEWER   You mentioned that the ISS is already over budget. Will this affect the estimated time of completion?

RICHTER   Yes, unfortunately, it will, in a way. Initially, they had hoped to be able to put as many as seven astronauts up there at any one time, but they're now going to be limited to three. **However,** we hope to have this smaller station complete by 2006.

INTERVIEWER   Well, Dr. Richter. That's all we've got time for today. Thank you for coming on the programme.

UNIT 7, EXTRACT 1

a

MAN

Heat always tends to move from places where there is a lot of heat to places where there is not quite so much. The transfer of heat from one place to another can be brought about in three ways, namely *conduction, convection* and *radiation.*

b

WOMAN

How intelligent are you? It's a question *psychologists* often ask, but now two mathematicians argue that it's meaningless. They say their experiments with computer 'mini-brains' prove that *intelligence* depends on the environment and can't exist independently of it. The work has reignited a fierce debate on the nature of *intelligence.*

c

MAN

Who were the first *astronomers*? Humans have always looked to the sky, trying to understand the *celestial* bodies that sweep across it. The ancient Greeks were the first to record their *observations*, and apply them to *calculate* the size of Earth and its *relativity* to the Moon and the Sun. Then, in the second century AD, Ptolemy concluded that Earth was the centre of the universe, a *philosophy* generally accepted for 1500 years.

d

WOMAN

We all have our image of the Amazon. For some it's a romantic place where the world's greatest river, its largest rainforest and its most diverse *ecosystems*, coexist in *harmony*. For others, it's a place echoing to the sound of chainsaws, turned to ashes by farmers and defiled by *mercury* spewing from gold mines.

e

MAN

A ballad is a narrative poem which tells a story – usually an exciting story – and one which also conveys an idea about the time in which it was written. Ballads date back hundreds of years to the days when books were rare; and so people would tell stories instead. Many of the first ballads told tales of courage, superstition and mystery.

f

WOMAN

It seems that languages have one single purpose – to communicate thought. Nevertheless, this aim is achieved in many different ways. As far as we can tell, there is no aspect of grammar or syntax that is universal or without which we cannot create language.

UNIT 7, EXTRACT 2

WOMAN

The famous scientist, Charles Darwin, *worked* and *worried* incessantly, so much so that he made himself ill. His wife, Emma, meanwhile, was *intelligent, liked literature* and not only did she *dance* gracefully, she *spoke French, German* and *Italian* well, and *played the piano* brilliantly.

Emma Darwin was born Emma Wedgwood – one of eight children from the well-to-do Wedgwood pottery family, famous to this day for their fine plates and chinaware. Charles was, in fact, her *first cousin* as his mother had also been a Wedgwood.

Emma coped well in society, whereas Charles did not. He *wasn't in the least bit interested in music,* nor did he have time to read anything but science. Nevertheless, by all accounts Emma made a *successful and happy* career out of the *marriage* and gave birth to *ten children* between the years 1839 and 1856. Her life has been documented in a recently published biography called 'Behind every great man' and we are pleased to welcome the author to our studio today.

UNIT 7, EXTRACT 3

a   MAN   Who was Ptolemy?
Do you know who Ptolemy was?

b   WOMAN   When were the pyramids built?
Can you tell me when the pyramids were built?

UNIT 7, EXTRACT 4

MAN

Good morning, everybody. Now last week we were looking at the positive effects that computers have had on our society. This week I'd like to talk about one of the negatives – computer viruses.

OK. So what is a computer virus? Well, it is a software program that has been designed, tested and released by a human programmer with the single intention of corrupting and destroying useful programs. Put in simple terms, it's a way of causing lots of trouble for ordinary people, just to be a nuisance! It's known as a virus because, *although it's not a biological organism, it functions in a similar way*, in that it seeks out a host; that is, a body, in which to live and multiply – your computer – with the end result of destroying that host.

Let's go back 50 years. In 1949 in the early days of computer technology, John Van Neumann *presented the first model* of a computer virus program in his paper 'Theory and Organization of Complicated Automata' 1949. Soon after this paper was published, we find reference to a game known as 'Core Wars'. Core Wars was initially created for intellectual entertainment *by three Americans* working on large *mainframe* computers. Remember, in those days computers were the size of a couple of rooms. By the 1980s for the small sum of $2.00 postage anyone could get details on how to play 'Core Wars' and very soon after, we see the *emergence of a new pastime*; one where people spent time creating programs that could escape the game and destroy other programs. In this way, the first computer viruses were born.

Like their biological counterparts, computer *viruses are picked up through casual habits*. Virus programs are often intentionally placed within useful programs in the public domain, or they're included in software which is not official – that is software that you might have acquired on the black market, which, of course you don't do!

It seems quite hard to believe that anyone would go to this level of deceit to intentionally corrupt the data of others, but the rise in the number of computer software infections, and the amount of lost data that we are seeing these days, *is proof that these virus programmers are going to extremes to do just that*. They are *going out of their way* to create programs that hide inside legitimate software applications and cause all sorts of errors that the average end-user will then mistake for hardware failure – in other words they will think that the problem lies with their own computer.

So, what can we do to combat these people? Well, the first thing is to realise that virus programmers succeed because people are not always careful about where they get their programs from. So – number one – *be very careful*. And I don't just mean that you should be careful about the source of your software, you also need to take care with e-mails and avoid any messages which are suspicious-looking. For instance a message that says 'I love you' or

'Win $50'. So the second golden rule is '*avoid trouble*'. Now there are other things we can do to protect ourselves. We can try to find out exactly how the viruses work, how they accomplish their aims – in other words, we need to *understand them*.

And, of course, there is a good selection of anti-virus software available on the market now as well as on the Internet to combat the virus plague, so another way of protecting ourselves and our computers is to *be well prepared*. And before I leave you, let me just say that if you ever run into one of those virus guys, tell them what you think of them!

UNIT 7, EXTRACT 5

WOMAN

Harnessing the Sun's energy, that is, using the sun to generate power, can be difficult, but these days increasing use *is* being made of the energy from the sun, particularly to heat homes and provide hot water. In particular, we are seeing an increase in the use of individualised heating units to serve the needs of individual households. Have a look at this diagram. It represents solar panels which are fixed to the roof of a house to 'capture', if you like, the sun's energy. It is typical of any system which uses a solar panel to provide hot water.

So how does it work? Well…energy from the Sun travels to the Earth in the form of radiation. This can be visible radiation, which is another way of saying 'light'. We also receive invisible radiation which is known as infra red. A lot of this radiation passes through the glass at the front of the *solar panel* – here on the roof – and hits the surface at the back. This surface is black because black is good at absorbing radiation and so the black surface becomes hot. Energy in the form of heat is conducted along the back of the solar panel to these *copper pipes*. Now…these pipes are filled with a liquid which in turn becomes hot. This can be either *oil or water*, though oil is usually used. The oil expands and rises up the pipe into the energy exchanger which is located – up here – in the *water tank*. Sometimes we have to use a *pump* as well to help the liquid along. It's a remarkably efficient system, when you think about it.

SPEAKING UNIT 1, EXTRACT 1

WOMAN

Yes, well…I grew up in a city called Victoria. It's the capital of the State of British Columbia, in Canada. It's actually not on the mainland but on a large island just to the west of Vancouver, called Vancouver Island. 'Cos in fact, just to confuse everyone, Vancouver itself is not on Vancouver Island but on the mainland.

Victoria has a pretty good climate…usually quite warm and certainly much better than the eastern states of Canada. I think it's a great place to grow up…not too big, not too small with some really lovely architecture. And the island itself is just so beautiful, once you get out of the city, that is.

These days the island is pretty famous for its eco-tourism…in particular whale watching –the best time to see the whales is from May to September, so lots of tourists come to the island in summer. I think Victoria is popular predominantly because it's safe…clean…and, of course, the people are very friendly. If you go to Victoria you have to visit the gardens, called the Butchart gardens…even if you're not really into gardens, you just have to go there.

MAN

I was born in *Melbourne*, in Victoria. *Victoria is a State in South East Australia.* Melbourne is a really Victorian city, with lots of *fine examples of 19th century architecture.* We're very proud of all our civic buildings and the way the city is, like…laid out. You know, with *wide streets* and avenues.

We're also very proud of our *trams.* Not like Sydney…which got rid of its trams in the 60s. Melbourne has always kept the trams and this gives the city a kind of…well, a kind of European feel. In fact…*my grandfather was a tram driver.*

There's always been a lot of rivalry between Melbourne and Sydney, and…well…I s'pose they are very different. We like to think we're…you know…a bit *more elegant* in Melbourne,… *smarter clothes, better restaurants*, that sort of thing! But the climate is pretty extreme! *In the summer it can be incredibly hot…35*, even 40 degrees Celsius. And in the winter, well… *it's often freezing.* Because there's nothing really much between us and Antarctica. And …*we even have our own little penguins…*to prove it!

SPEAKING UNIT 1, EXTRACT 2

WOMAN

I grew up in a city called Victoria.

It's the capital of the State of British Columbia, in Canada.

Victoria has a pretty good climate…usually quite warm and certainly much better than the eastern states of Canada.

I think it's a great place to grow up…not too big, not too small with some really lovely architecture.

And the island itself is just so beautiful, once you get out of the city, that is.

I think Victoria is popular, predominantly because it's safe… clean…and, of course, the people are very friendly.

SPEAKING UNIT 1, EXTRACT 3

island	whale watching
climate	wide streets
architecture	a European feel
19th century architecture	eco-tourism
popular	breathtakingly
restaurants	predominantly
friendly	certainly
rivalry	incredibly

SPEAKING UNIT 2, EXTRACT 1

TEENAGER (BOY)	I really like rock music. These days you can find a lot of good music on the Internet. And that's fantastic!
WOMAN	I really only listen to classical music and opera. To be honest with you, I find modern music quite unbearable. It's just a terrible noise as far as I'm concerned.
TEENAGER (GIRL)	Actually, my favourite kind of music is film music. I enjoy listening to the sound tracks of movies – especially when I've really enjoyed the film.

SPEAKING UNIT 2, EXTRACT 2

MAN

I just love skiing. I've been doing it since I was six years old so it comes pretty naturally to me now. But it can be dangerous for people who take it up later in life. And yes, it's pretty common for people to get quite badly injured – you know – broken arms and legs. In particular knee injuries are really common and they can be quite nasty. Or you can easily run into a tree, or get lost in the snow, if you aren't careful. All part of the fun!

But … you know what I love about skiing is the solitude…the challenge of the mountain. There's nothing anywhere near as exhilarating as the feeling you get when you're hurtling down the side of a mountain – the sense of freedom is amazing – just you against nature. It beats any team sport…in my opinion.

WOMAN

Well…my favourite sport is *rowing.* I row in an *eight.* There are *eight of us in the boat*, plus the cox who steers the boat…and shouts at us a lot! It's really *hard work* when you first start, 'cos you get terrible *blisters on your hands…*and your *muscles really ache*, especially your leg muscles. And you have to *get up at 4.30 in the morning* to be on the water by five, but after a few weeks, you get used to that. Most of my friends think I'm mad and I know they say: 'What does she see in this?' But, you know…it's such a *good feeling* being out on the water early in the morning. And when we're working well together…you know, all eight of us working really well as a team…it's just a marvellous *sense of satisfaction. And the best thing of all is winning!*

SPEAKING UNIT 3, EXTRACT 1

WOMAN

Melbourne zoo is probably one of the best zoos I've ever been to…and I'm not that keen on zoos normally…because it's a very open zoo. It's near the centre of the city, next to the Botanical Gardens, and it's really worth a visit.

I actually went there with my family – with my husband and the children during the last school holidays…and…they were very impressed because, for instance, you can see the lions from a bridge – you walk across the top of them and they appear to be quite free, roaming around underneath you. So were the elephants …in fact, they are separated by a kind of moat, which has water in it, and it means that they can't get across it but the impression that you have is that the animals are actually quite free.

The zoo has a great variety of animals and you can see all sorts of creatures from all over the world, though of course, a particular emphasis on Australia…on Australian animals. One interesting thing is that they've kept an old 19th century building, originally built as a monkey cage, as a reminder of how the zoo used to be. But these days the monkeys have a much better enclosure and the zoo prides itself on its humanitarian approach. I think it's probably one of the best zoos in the world.

SPEAKING UNIT 3, EXTRACT 2

MAN

Many years ago when I was in South Africa, I visited a wildlife park called Timbavati, in Natal Province. I went with my two aunts and my sister and we flew into the park in a small plane from Johannesburg, north east, and as we were landing on the strip we had to take off again because there was a giraffe on the strip. It was so exciting being there. There were no modern buildings; we just had one guide and there were six other people with us and we lived in little mud huts for four days – it was really exciting. We felt as though we were completely on our own although we had the security of having a guard with a gun. He said he'd never had to use it! I felt very privileged to be there with all the animals around us and only six other people besides us. The guard took us out at dawn and then again at dusk, 'cos that's when you're most likely to see the animals. We also went out at night, once or twice, and that was really amazing – quite frightening though, because you'd see all these little eyes all around you…peering at you. We saw lions, elephants, giraffes, gazelle, everything. It was absolutely marvellous.

SPEAKING UNIT 5, EXTRACT 1

a

WOMAN   I believe there are a number of good reasons for keeping animals in a zoo. One is that you can see animals from other countries; animals you would never see in the wild. And zoos are really great for children, 'cos they can have the chance to see unusual animals.

b

MAN   Personally, I don't like zoos. I can't see the point in them. You can see animals on the television, if that's what you want.

c

WOMAN   Well, I can see a number of benefits. Firstly they give us the chance to observe animal behaviour and they also help us protect certain species of animal, like the panda bear, for instance. Animals which may be under threat in the wild.

d

MAN   I'm afraid I can't see any real benefits – at least not in the case of zoos. Though I may be wrong … Wildlife parks, on the other hand, are probably more useful, because they can actually help to protect animals from poachers or when there are environmental disasters such as drought.

e

WOMAN   I tend to think zoos can be of enormous benefit. But not just so that we can see rare and exotic beasts, or animals, but because they are … they act as a kind of research laboratory. But if I had my way, I'd probably keep the people out of the zoos – just keep them for the animals!

f

MAN   There may be good things for us – humans. But I can't see what the poor animals get out of it. I mean, would you want to be stuck in a cage all day?

g

WOMAN   I think the benefits of keeping animals in a zoo are that we can see animals such as lions and tigers, or kangaroos which you wouldn't normally see. Well, not where I come from, anyway. But some people think it's really cruel, and they may have a point.

Answer Key

Listening Unit 1

Extract 1
1 a 2 c 3 g 4 j 5 h 6 l 7 i
8 b 9 e 10 f

Extract 2
11 Full meal
12 $15
13 ✓✓
14 Science Café
15 $5
16 ✗
17 Bread Basket
18 Sandwich
19 $8-10 / $8 to $10
20 ?

Listening Unit 2

Extract 1
1 C

Extract 2
2 B 3 A

Extract 3
4 B / D

Extract 4
5 C 6 B 7 A 8 C 9 A 10 C 11 B
12 B ⎫
13 E ⎬ in any order
14 F ⎭
15 What does the man want to study? Type 2. A subject or discipline.
16 When was Louis Pasteur born? Where was Louis Pasteur born ? Type 2. A date or place.
17 How much does a concession ticket cost? Type 1. A number, price.
18 What is the address? Type 1. Name of street.
19 What was the reason for the delay? Type 1. A reason or explanation.
20 How many gallons of water do New Yorkers use each day? Type 2. A number.
21 When does...arrive? Type 1. A date.
22 What were the early navigators unable to do? Type 2. An action or process.
23 What type of car is it? Type 1. Manufacturer's name or model of car.
24 What are spring rolls made from? Type 2. Ingredients.

Extract 5
25 18–20 October / 18th to 20th October
26 (the) Pacific Hotel
27 07 9333 2233
28 $60
29 Professor Dawson
30 last Friday
31 (an) interesting title
32 300 words
33 short CV/brief CV/short Curriculum Vitae
34 admin (small letters)

Listening Unit 3

Extract 1
Sample notes
1 Origins of the game; Similar game played in Japan & China in 1000 BC
2 Most famous player; Pelé – Brazilian – won World Cup 3 times – national hero
3 Rules of the game; Date from 1815 – FIFA changes the rules sometimes
4 History of the World Cup; First played in 1930. Won by Uruguay. Most watched sport.
5 First football leagues; Formed in 1888 in England. Matches played between the leagues. Other countries followed suit.

Extract 2
6 (northern) India
7 2000
8 rules
9 China
10 1400
11 (chess) pieces
12 sand clock
13 official champion / official world champion / official chess champion
14 top three players
15 American / native-born American / native-born US citizen

Listening Unit 4

Extract 1

Conversation	Speakers?	Where are they?	Topic or purpose of conversation?	Phrasal verb(s) used	Meaning of phrasal verbs in this context
1 *Example*	*Shop assistant and customer*	*in clothes shop*	*Assistant attempting to make a sale*	*to try on*	*to put clothes on to see if they fit*
2	Student & librarian	Library	Student wants to borrow a book	I'*m after*	I want, I'm in need of
3	Customer & shop assistant	Shop	Customer wants a particular item	We'*re out of*	We haven't got any more in stock.
4	Customer & bookshop assistant	Bookshop	Customer wants a book	Let me *look it up*. I'm *looking for*	try to find it in a catalogue, dictionary or list
5	Receptionist & student	Phone to University medical centre	Student wants to make an appointment	The doctors are *booked up*.	There are no vacancies or appointments available.
6	Student & nurse	Hospital – Casualty Department	Student wants to see a doctor	to *fill out* this form	complete the form
7	Woman student & lecturer	Lecturer's room	Student is seeking more time to complete an essay	I've *run into* a problem to *get hold of*	I have a problem to find or locate
8	Student & student (friend)	Phone to friend's house	Friend is inviting the other one to join him	(I may as well) *give up* Economics	stop doing the course
9	Student & student	University or social setting	Friends discussing their plans	it *cut into* my time *signing up* *give up* all your Saturdays	It took a lot of my time joining / taking part in sacrifice your time
10	Student & bank teller	Bank	Customer transaction	*pay off* my overdraft	pay the amount owing to clear the debt

Extract 2

11 C
12 fast/quick(ly) flowing/moving
13 straight line / course
14 poles (in river)
15 skier / skiing
16 Scotland / Wales (must have both)
(Phrasal verbs highlighted in canoeing script, see recording script)

17 £300 / £700 (must have both)
18 wet(-)suit
19 B
20 A

to take up — to become interested in a sport or pastime
to catch on — to become popular
to set you back — to cost s.o. an amount of money
to look at — to consider
to be put off — to be discouraged
to look for — to seek out

Listening Unit 5

Extract 1

1 Marriage / 2 / Yes / I think so too; In my opinion, that's just too young, isn't it?
2 Studies / 2 / Yes / I'm finding it…to tell you the truth; Yes,…I feel the same about…
3 Space, Iss / 2 / No / I can't think of anything worse.
4 Water / 2 / Yes / I know. That's right.
5 Education / 3 / No / I'm not so sure about that.
6 Art gallery / 3 / No and Yes / I thought it was great; Frankly…I prefer…; I think it's quite a good idea really.
7 Politics, elections / 3 / No and Yes / I agree with Sarah; I think we need a change
8 (shopping) Survey / 2 / No / Don't you think…?; I would have thought it was.
9 Sport in newspapers / 3 / No / Just because…; I just think…; I think Susan's got a point.
10 Music / 2 / No / Intonation in 'What is that music you're listening to?'; implying that she does not like it; Can't you play…?

Extract 2

A Bookshop	2 buying a book.
B Radio or TV programme	2 sport
C Tutorial setting	3 children & TV
D Lecture	2 environment
E Radio or TV programme	2 space research, science

Extract 3

11 (completely) natural / virgin bush
12 4 years
13 cats and foxes / (feral, domestic) cats
14 farmers / miners
15 A **16** C **17** B **18** A **19** B **20** C

Listening Unit 6

Extract 1

Most appropriate use
a *Even though* – signals an opposite
b *On top of everything else* – signals an additional negative point
c *Finally* – indicates the speaker is making one last point
d *No matter what* – signals a definite statement
e *As a result of* – indicates a cause and effect relationship
f *Not only* – signals an additional related point (followed by but)
g *For example* – signals a detail illustrating the main point

Extract 2

1 C **2** B **3** A
4 C ⎫
5 E ⎬ in any order
6 F ⎭
7 C ⎫
8 E ⎬ in any order
9 joined together / connected
10 food and electricity / food and power

Listening Unit 7

Extract 1

1

-tion / shun/	-ology / -ologist
conduction convection radiation observations superstition mathematician	psychologist philosophy

-ent / -ence	Others
intelligent experiment intelligence environment independently mysterious multiplicity	a'stronomer ce'lestial 'calculate 'ecosystems rela'tivity 'harmony 'mercury 'narrative 'newspapers super'stition co'mmunicate neverthe'less uni'versal

2 You stress the second syllable from the end in words ending in /shun/ and the third syllable from the end in words that have these other endings.

Extract 2

3

	Key words	Main focus
1	Charles: worked; worried Emma: intelligent, liked literature, danced, spoke languages, played piano	Emma's abilities
2	Emma and Charles cousins	Her background
3	C hated music, E happy marriage 10 children	Contrast between them

Extract 3

4

Do you know who *Ptolemy* was? (Focus on Ptolemy as opposed to Archimedes, for example.)
Do you know *who* Ptolemy was? (Focus on the identity of the person.)
Do *you* know who Ptolemy was? (Focus on the person being asked the question.)
Do *know* who Ptolemy was? (Suggesting the person being asked may not know.)
Do you know who Ptolemy was? (Suggesting the question is important.)

Can you tell me *when* the pyramids were built? (Focus on the date.)
Can you tell me when the *pyramids* were built? (Focus on the pyramids, as opposed to another structure.)
Can *you* tell me when the pyramids were built? (Focus on the person being asked the question.)
Can you tell me when the pyramids were built? (Showing surprise that the listener can.)
Can you *tell* me when the pyramids were built? (Implying irritation on the part of the speaker.)

Extract 4

5 A   **10** B
6 first model **11** be (very) careful
7 (three) Americans **12** avoid trouble
8 mainframe   **13** understand them / viruses
9 pastime   **14** be (well) prepared

Extract 5

15 solar panel
16 copper pipe
17 oil or water (must have both)
18 water tank
19 pump

Reading Unit 1

1 Topic: (old) (colour) photographs
Main idea: are fading/are changing (because of the way their dyes break down)
2 Topic: animation *or* computer-generated motion
Main idea: characters must look real

3 B

4 **e** Darwin is a large telescope that has recently been built to observe nearby stars.

f Scientists have discovered some unexpected facts about humour.

g The strength of the Internet is also its weakness.

5 **i)** d **ii)** c **iii)** d, f **iv)** e, g **v)** d, b

6 B

7 guidebook – a book that provides information to visitors
shelf-life – the period during which a product can be sold
non-problematic – straightforward
backpacker – someone who travels with a pack/rucksack on their back

8 (Topic: travel/guidebooks
Main idea: outdated, there may be as much as four years between the original research and a tourist's visit)
Summary sentence: There are various factors that may lead to the unreliability of guidebooks.

9   era

10 based

11 susceptible

12 target

13 easier said than done

14 at random

15 fair/good chance

16 truly perplexing

Further practice
Collect some articles and underline the topic and main idea. Try writing a summary sentence of some of the paragraphs.

Reading Unit 2

1 South Carolina

2 John Sadler

3 Leafsen

4 Israel

5 peppers/tomatoes/grapefruit

6 sensor

7 thickness

8 computer

9 processor

10 **a** holds the key – is the solution to

b multinational corporations – huge international companies whose owners and operations are in more than one country

c vaccines – a substance used to produce antibodies and provide immunity against particular diseases

d solar energy – power obtained by using the energy of the sun's rays

e developing countries – poor agricultural countries which are trying to become more advanced economically and socially

f tropical diseases – diseases which are widespread in countries with hot and humid climates

g socially responsible – actively working to help the poor, and developing countries

h take into acccount – consider a specified thing along with other factors before making a decision

i genetically modified crops – crops grown commercially from seeds which have had their genetic characteristics changed, e.g. to produce more

j revolutionise – change something radically or fundamentally

11 The name of a printed text e.g. a book or newspaper.

12 A number.

13 South Africa.

14 Two answers are needed for one mark.

15 2 billion

16 United Nations report

17 multinationals / big corporations

18 1223

19 intellectual property laws

20 genetically modified crops

21 Brazil (and) India

22 If it is easy to save lives, what is stopping us from doing it now?

23 This question is about the recommended production of genetically modified crops. Western countries produce these crops so developing countries should have them too.

Reading Unit 3

g Introduces the main focus of the passage

a Lexical link between POD and 'This latest abbreviation'.

d Lexical link 'store' and grammatical link; the present perfect continuous tense is often used to refer back to something that has been done and that then leads on to something else. Here 'it is possible to store the text', links up with 'Having been stored …'

f 'Not only that' is used to add a further point to an argument. Here it is adding another advantage of electronic books.

e 'All the advantages' refers back to paragraphs d and f.

b Lexical link between 'this problem' and 'the worrying thing'.

c 'For' indicates that an earlier point is going to be explained further. Also, 'most in danger' refers back to the 'problem'.

h Link between the final sentence of c and 'such measures'. This paragraph also contains the concluding point.

The following words would be suitable in a title and or subheading: publishing, books, technology, concerns, future.

1 But, however, although.

2 A pronoun referring back to the noun 'profits'.

3 At the same time.

4 Moreover.

5 A supporting argument to the first sentence.

6 'Even' highlights surprise. Hollywood movies on this topic would only result from extreme public sentiment.

7 Line 33. No. Here it is adding emphasis to the comparative. ('Hostility' links back to 'dissatisfaction'.)

8 To cap it all...

9 One answer is...

10 Question 17

11 Question 15

12 Questions 13 and 14

13 C 'two contrasting trends' (understanding the reference helps you answer this question)

14 D 'airlines are having to work harder and harder for them' (understanding what 'them' refers back to helps you do this question)

15 B Signalled by the use of 'even'.

16 B 'Contributing to global warming...'
D 'The rise in the number of flights...'
E 'Sitting for long periods... can cause blood clots.'

17 B The first question and the phrase that follows suggest reasons will be given. These are not excuses as the writer makes the point in the last sentence of this paragraph that the system could work better.

18 however

19 even

20 in response to this

21 at the same time

22 to cap it all (best inserted after 'Then')

23 **a** People who will be alive in the future.

b Organisations that publish printed texts or music.

c Companies that own or operate a fleet of aeroplanes or aircraft.

d People who use some form of transport but do not drive it.

e *example*

f Any ordinary person who purchases an air ticket.

g Everyone/anybody who is a member of society.

h People who try to protect the environment from being damaged by human activities.

i People who pay money for goods or services.

Reading Unit 4

1 B

2 C

3 Main idea.

4 Further explanation/details of noosphere.

5 Topic.

6 To introduce the idea that museums have far more exhibits behind the scenes than on show.

7 To emphasise the main idea, i.e. the high number of exhibits that museums contain.

8 The first sentence.

9 The size and breadth of the collections.

10 Either to allow classification of things found in nature or to highlight changes over time.

11 All the collections referred to so far.

12 Museum collections are getting larger and, as a result, more and more items are being stored behind the scenes. However, this means that a smaller percentage of museum contents are on display to the general public, which is a disadvantage. In order to retain public and government support, therefore, museum curators are keen to show as many of their back-room items as possible but this is not always easy to do.

13 Refer to page 43 of *Insight into IELTS*.

14 'unsafe'

15 **v** 'On an international scale, however, such numbers are not exceptional.'

16 **xi** 'The huge, invisible collections behind the scenes at science and natural history museums are the result of the dual functions of these institutions.'

17 **vi** 'The museum is also custodian to things that are dangerous...'

18 **x** 'Neil Brown... spends his professional life looking for objects that illustrate some aspect of scientific and technological development. But the rapid pace of technological change, and the volume of new objects, makes it increasingly hard to identify what future generations will regard as significant.'

19 **i** 'The public is often surprised at the Science Museum's interest in recent objects.'

20 **ii** 'Natural history museums collect for a different reason.' Some of the plants and animals they hold are "type specimens". 'Other specimens are valuable because of their age.'

21 **iv** 'Year after year, the value of such collections quietly and reliably increases, as scientists find uses that would have been unimaginable to those who started them a century or two ago.'

22 **viii** 'But museums that show the public only a small fraction of their material risk losing the fickle goodwill of governments and the public, which they need to keep running. Hence the determination of so many museums to make their back room collections more widely available.'

23 a big job / A / a monumental task

globally / B / an international scale

these large collections / B / these huge accumulations of things

a difficult task / B / a pressing problem

a small part / B / a tiny fraction

the two roles / C / the dual functions (of these institutions)

the main place where things are kept / D / principal storage facility

his work time / E / his professional life

the fast speed / E / the rapid pace

people alive in the next 100 years or so / E / future generations

the year 2000 / E / the turn of the century

Reading Unit 5

1 Paragraph 1: 'As a product, chocolate has a lot going for it, appealing to all ages, both sexes and all income brackets.'

2 Paragraph 2: 'It also increasingly transcends national boundaries.'

3 Paragraph 3: 'Media expenditure on confectionery exceeds that for any other impulse market.'

4 Paragraph 4: 'Innovation is also essential for ongoing success, despite the chocolate market being dominated by consistent performers.'

5 Paragraph 5: 'Producers believe that special editions offer the consumer a new and exciting variation of a product.'

6 It covers the first two paragraphs.

7 It is testing facts.

8 £3.6bn

9 100 countries

10 Asia

11 American

12 a third

13 well-known

14 media

15 new

16 purchasing

17 outdated

18 temporary

19 novelty

20 overall

21 It covers the last three paragraphs.

22 It is testing ideas and facts.

23 Paragraph 1: For this reason, In fact
Paragraph 2: However, one example of this, also, For example, this
Paragraph 3: These, also

24
a *example*

b	market	marketing executive, etc.	the (product/country) market
c	sell	seller/ salesperson	good/poor sales/sales growth
d	grow	grower	fast/slow growth
e	retail	retailer	retail trade/industry
f	brand	–	brand image
g	industrialise	industrialist	the (product) industry
h	stock	stockist	check stock/ stock-taking
i	launch	–	product launch

Reading Unit 6

A The research question: Do Apes ape?
B A type of behaviour that could be copied. Those who do not believe that apes copy behaviour.
C Chimpanzee culture and its definition.
D One type of experiment that was conducted (on different subjects).
E It describes another type of experiment (in differing environments).
F That chimpanzees rate observation above intuition.
G The writers' conclusions and some justification for these.
H To make some concessions but re-assert the conclusion.

1 G 'ant-dipping and parasite-handling'
2 D 'three-year-old children' and 'chimpanzees'
3 C 'Some scientists define a cultural trait as...'
4 A See the title and by-line above.
5 E 'zoos' and 'the wild'
6 F Paragraph B: 'as has been observed....'
7 A Paragraph B: 'They argue that...' prefaces this point so it is not a fact.
8 A Paragraph C: 'Some scientists define...' prefaces this point so it is not a fact but a view.
9 F Paragraph G: This is an observation during an experiment so it is a fact: 'only after several viewings'
10 F These are presented as facts in paragraph G.
11 A 'the question of whether apes really do "ape", has become controversial'
D 'although the fidelity of their copying tends to be poorer'
F 'learning from elders is crucial to growing up as a competent wild chimpanzee'
12 controversial / adjective / causing disagreement or discussion
sceptics / noun / people who doubt the truth of certain ideas
distinction / noun / clear difference
implications / noun / future effects
exclusively / adverb / solely / in no other way
collaboration / noun / the act of working together, e.g. on a joint project
imitative / adjective / based on copying

monitored / verb / observe behaviour over a period of time
converge / verb / move towards the same point (of agreement)
crucial / adjective / most important / critical

Reading Unit 7

1 Make a debut.
2 Find wanting.
3 Be on shaky ground.
4 The upshot.
5 Hold in awe (be in awe of).
6 The/a turning point.
7 Rough and ready.
8 Cast doubt on.
9 held my English Professor in such awe / was so in awe of my English Professor
10 rough and ready
11 cast (serious) doubt on
12 made their debut
13 The turning point in Jim's career came when
14 (now) found his friends' company wanting
15 What jury…
16 Surprisingly.
17 This is not to say that...
18 That puts fingerprinting...
19 Refer to page 55 of *Insight into IELTS*.
20 NO questions state the opposite of what is stated in the passage. In NOT GIVEN questions, you cannot find any information in the passage that is related to the question.
21 YES **22** NO **23** NO **24** NO **25** YES
26 NOT GIVEN **27** YES
28 enjoy / enhance / uphold
29 increase / give
30 carry out
31 give / raise / enhance / uphold
32 raise
33 carry out
34 subject (to)
35 back up
36 give / uphold
37 raised, been carried out
38 uphold, enhance
39 carried out, upheld
40 subjected to, increase
41 back up, enjoy

Reading Unit 8

1 in Antibes / in France
2 Picasso
3 Wednesdays and holidays
4 June – September / June to September
5 you request one/you ask
6 three / 3
7 the harbour
8 nothing
9 use a flash

10 Christmas Day

11 True		17 True	
12 False		18 False	
13 False		19 Not given	
14 Not given		20 False	
15 True		21 Not given	
16 Not given		22 True	

Reading Unit 9

1 iii   2 vi   3 ii   4 v   5 viii   6 i

7 discipline	13 degree
8 guidelines	14 reimbursement
9 assignment	15 research
10 semester	16 to enrol
11 department	17 exhibition
12 co-ordinator	

18 enrol	22 assignments
19 co-ordinator	23 degree
20 semester	24 research
21 department	25 guidelines

26 F   27 D   28 B   29 C   30 E   31 A   32 A
33 E   34 F

Writing Unit 1

1 It should be 1,123 million speakers.

2 It should be 121 million speakers and German is *not* the least-spoken language in the world.

3
a Russian	g second
b most	h 125 million
c 1,123 million	i higher
d second	j least
e 470 million	k relatively
f widely	

4 nouns: student / course / subject / degree / increase / fall / drop
adjectives: full-, part-time / fewer / less / more / biggest
verbs: take up / increase / go up / fall / opt / choose
adverbs: significantly / relatively
phrases: just over / slightly more than

5 *example*

6 Just under 20,000 full-time students enrolled in the Mathematical sciences in 2002.

7 Sixty thousand...

8 ...went down/fell by...

9 ...the part-time enrolments in Education courses fell / dropped by twelve per cent.

10 In 2002...there was no change in the number of enrolments on...

11 ...in the number of full-time enrolments...

12 The pie chart provides a clear visual image of how the total responses divide into age-groups. The table provides more detailed information on actual numbers.

13 viewers / (in the) age-group / total / largest / second-largest / smallest / represent / comprise

14 Sentences 3 and 4 and the final comment.

15 A total of 1,510 people said they watched the soap opera. Just over half these people were in the 21–25

age-group which comprised a total of 758 viewers. This was the largest age-group. Seventeen per cent of the viewers were in the second-largest age-group (26–30), which had a total of 258 people. There was a similar number of viewers aged below 20. After the age of 30, the number of viewers fell significantly. The 31–35 age-group made up only 10 per cent of the viewers and there were 76 people in the 36–40 age-group who said they watched the programme. Only three per cent of the viewers were over 40. Obviously the programme appeals to young people most.

16 The graph compares trends in population growth in China and India.

17 The graph shows the number of vehicles sold worldwide.

18 The chart provides information on the number of doctors per thousand of the population, in selected countries.

19 An athlete's diet should consist of large quantities of carbohydrate.
In fact, 60 per cent of an athlete's daily diet should be made up of carbohydrates.
The second most important food group is fat which should account for 25 per cent of an athlete's diet.
The food group which is required in the smallest amounts is protein.
The appropriate proportion of this food group is 15 per cent of the total food intake.

Writing Unit 2

1 1998, 2002

2 a steady increase, between 1998 and 2002

3 4 billion, 1998, 80 billion, 2002

4 Average attendance at NBA matches in America has remained fairly stable since 1996 at 17000 spectators per game. (Although) attendance at Dallas Maverick games dropped sharply between 1996 and 1998, it has risen equally sharply since then and is now almost equal to the NBA average.

5 Membership at Jay's Sports Club rose during the first three months of last year from 50 to approximately 120. Between March and August this figure remained stable but in September there was a sudden rise in membership numbers, which reached a peak of 175 in October. After that, figures fell again to a low of 100 in December.

6 a lot of, considerable, wide

7 electricity consumption

8 During the course of a televised World Cup football match electricity consumption fluctuates widely / undergoes considerable fluctuation.

9 At the start of the match, demand for electricity stands at about 28,500 units.
There is a significant fall in demand during the first hour of the match but then the demand rises steeply and peaks at 29,000 units at half time.
Demand falls again quite sharply at the start of the second half and hits its lowest point at 26,000 units.
In the last forty minutes of the match, electricity

consumption increases steadily to just over 28,000 units. However, at the beginning of the extra-time period consumption falls dramatically, hits a low plateau and then immediately rises to resume normal consumption levels at the end of this period.

10 It lacks an introductory paragraph/sentence: The number of Japanese students attending university has risen steadily since 1960. At that time, a very small percentage of women went to university and just under 15 per cent of men received a university education, whereas nowadays, these figures are significantly higher.

11 **a** increase   **e** smaller   **i** fall
    b consistent   **f** fluctuation   **j** trends
    c risen   **g** rose   **k** parallels
    d steeply   **h** high

Writing Unit 3

1 Birth rates.
2 Children per family.
3 Decrease in birth rates in developing countries.
4 The projected birth rates for 2050.
5 The dates cover past, present and future.
6 Population in billions.
7 The population growth rate is slowing up.
8 Key points on graph when trend changes.
9 Forecasts (later than graph 1).
10 The overall population growth rate – the second graph.
11 The data in first graph accounts for trend in second graph.
12 The decrease in birth rates in developing countries.
13 The projections show growth rates will be the same/low in all areas of the world.
14 **a** Gives an overall description of what the graphs show.
    b Describes the trend in second graph.
    c Links the data in second graph to statistics in first graph.
    d Describes the trend in the developing world.
    e Describes the trend in the developed world.
15 Sedentary activities are more popular than physical ones / the most popular activities involve sitting at a screen.
16 Rank the activities in terms of popularity.
17 are far more popular nowadays than; the second most popular activity; While girls … – just under 60% … –

only 35% of boys …; on the other hand; almost as popular as; relatively less popular

18 The chart shows the percentage change in enrolment figures, between the years 2001 and 2002, at one university. During this period, Arts, Humanities and Language courses were generally less popular than Science courses (although there were some variations on this). Part-time enrolments on these courses fell considerably and full-time enrolments fell or changed very little.
Overall, part-time enrolments stayed below 20,000 for all subject areas. As for full-time enrolments the most heavily subscribed subject areas were Business (around 100,000 students) and Engineering (just over 80,000 students).
A significant increase in student enrolments occurred in the Biological sciences: full-time enrolments went up by nine per cent and part-time enrolments, by five per cent. There was also a considerable increase in the number of part-time students signing up for Mathematical sciences; at 11 per cent, this was the single most significant increase, although overall, student numbers were the lowest at just under 1,000 for part-time students and just under 20,000 full-timers.

19 **a** The graph shows how Mexico's import of fuel products changed over a ten-year period. The value of Mexico's total import of energy-based products increased markedly from $500m in 1990 to $2billion in the year 2000.
    b Despite some fluctuation, imports of natural gas grew over the period and in 2000, expenditure on this product reached approximately $1,250m.
    c This is a far greater amount than that spent on diesel and natural gas.
    d Expenditure on these fuels remained under $500m.
    e An equal amount was spent on natural gas in 2000 although the pattern of growth was slightly different over the ten-year period.
20 The cost in pounds per week and the salary in pounds per year.
21 A property with 2 bedrooms.
22 Suburb or district.
23 A three-bedroom house (NB no plural on bedroom).
24 To illustrate how much you need to earn to rent accommodation in London.

IELTS task page 79 sample answer

The table shows two sets of related information: the relative cost, in pounds, of renting a property with one, two or three bedrooms in three different suburbs of London and an indication of the kind of annual salary you would need to be earning to rent in these areas.	*Tells the reader what they will learn from the table.*
Of the three areas mentioned, Notting Hill is the most expensive with weekly rents starting at £375 (salary approximately £100,000) and rising to £738 per week for a 3-bedroom property. To afford this, you would require a salary in the region of £200,000 per annum. Alternatively, Fulham is the cheapest area shown with rents ranging from £215 per week for a one bedroom property to £600 per week for a 3-bedroom property. To rent in this area, salaries need to be somewhere between £85,000 and £170,000 depending on the number of bedrooms required. For those able to pay in the middle price range for accommodation, Regent's Park might be a more suitable district.	*Provides some details which illustrate the main thrust of the data but avoids quoting every detail.*

Writing Unit 4

1 The direction of the wind / a cause effect relationship.
2 Vegetation.
3 Heavy industries.
4 The present and present perfect tense used to describe an on-going process.
5 By following the stages in the process.
6 Initially, then, eventually.
7 The Hawaiian chain of islands and how they were/are formed.
8 Vocabulary related to volcanic activity; e.g. active / inactive; magma; erupt(ion).
9 A description of the mountain chain and where it is located.
10 The development of the first volcano.
11 Yes. The third paragraph could focus on the movement of the tectonic plate and the formation of the chain of volcanoes.
12 Paragraph 2 should come before paragraph 1.
13 2,883km in first paragraph and 7–9cm in last paragraph.
14 The first sentence in the second paragraph and the final sentence.
15 The second sentence in the second paragraph is not part of the description.
16 Here is a corrected version of the answer with the linkers in italics and a summary of the content of each paragraph.

The Hawaiian island chain, in the centre of the Pacific Ocean, is approximately 2,700 km in length. It is formed of volcanoes *and* the active ones are at the south-east tip of the archipelago, where Hawaii itself is located.	*Describes the subject or topic of the question.*
It is believed that the chain began to form nearly 80 million years ago. Each island started to evolve after an eruption on the sea floor. *First*, a 'hot spot' existed on the ocean bed, which let out a plume of material called magma. *This magma* may originate as deep as 2,883km below the ocean bed. *Next*, further eruptions took place, which built up the volcano. Eventually, it emerged above the surface of the ocean.	*Describes how a volcano is formed in the sea.*
Since that time, the spume of magma has remained static as the Pacific tectonic plate moves in a north-west direction across it at a speed of 7–9cm per year. *As it moves*, a volcano forms as it passes over the hotspot and *then* become inactive when it has passed it.	*Explains why a chain of active and inactive volcanoes has formed.*

IELTS task page 83 sample answer

The Eiffel Tower is situated close to the Seine River in Paris. It is a metal structure that is 1,063 feet high and weighs 7,417 tonnes. The tower has been a tourist attraction since 1889, when it was built, and there are 1,665 steps that can be climbed in order to reach the two viewing platforms.	*Describes the tower and what it is used for.*
There are now plans to build below the foundations of the tower. These plans include the development of five underground levels that will incorporate the tower's ticket office, shopping facilities, a cinema and museum and two floors of underground parking.	*Outlines the levels and what they will be used for.*
Although details have yet to be finalised, the principle is that the five floors will be connected by two vertical passenger lifts on either side of the tower. In addition, the floor immediately below the tower, which is planned to house the ticket office, will also consist of a large atrium with a glass ceiling so that visitors can look directly up at the tower itself.	*Gives further details of the construction.*

Writing Unit 5

1 company and job
taking the job
problems
solutions

2 Sample answer

Dear Sir,	*Explains why job was taken.*
I have been a part-time fitness instructor in your gym for four months. I was pleased to be offered the job, not only because I need to earn some extra money to cover my living expenses as a student, but also because I wanted some experience in fitness training.	
During these months, it has become obvious to me that people often need help in using the gym equipment. However, it seems that the other trainers have not been encouraged to offer assistance to club members. I offer as much as I can, but this means that I am constantly in demand and, therefore, working harder than anyone else in the gym. This situation seems rather unfair.	*Describes problems.*
While I realise that members receive initial gym instruction, I feel that they also need ongoing help with the equipment. Could I suggest that a letter is sent to trainers promoting this? After all, personal attention of this kind makes people feel valued and may result in increased membership.	*Suggests a solution. Closing sentence points out a benefit to the management.*

3 d, e and f: one-hour performance, no musical instruments, well-known songs (in any order)
g, h and i: good for all ages, very unusual, finishes next Monday (in any order)

4 The first sentence has been copied from the rubric and there are poor links between sentences, the material is not well organised.

5 Last Friday was my mother's birthday and so I decided to take her to the theatre to see a concert. A South African group were playing, called 'The Swing Band', and they put on a wonderful performance.

6 'Hot Jive' a Brazilian percussion band
Ticket from neighbour
Wasn't busy, so went along
Colourful clothes, scenery
Music – Jungle Rhythms – best, sounded like jungle
Lasted 15 minutes
Playing near her/him
Recommend he/she goes

IELTS task page 86 sample answer

Dear Sam,	*Explains where the place was and how she got there.*
I have just returned from my holidays in France and while we were there we climbed a mountain called 'Parmelan' in the French Alps. We were able to drive half way up the mountain but then the road stopped. So we parked, put on our walking boots and began the long uphill struggle.	
Despite the road at the beginning, it still took us a while to complete the climb but it was well worth the effort. When we got to the top of the mountain, the view was incredible. I could see right across the town and the lake to one side, and on the other side were the snow-covered peaks of Mont Blanc. It was simply breathtaking.	*Describes what she saw.*
As you know, we often go to France on our holidays and next time we plan a trip, I'd really like to take you there. I'm sure you would love the scenery and as you enjoy exercise, you would be able to take advantage of all the mountain walks.	*Offers to take friend.*

Writing Unit 6

1 Explain, give reasons for, apologise. These are the 'function' words which tell the candidate what they have to do in the letter. The task requires a letter of apology.

2 The third bullet, making the apology. It expresses emotions while the other two parts are explanatory.

3 a I cannot understand why
  b I feel confident...
  c We greatly appreciate...
  d We wonder whether it would be possible to....
  e Although....I did not feel sure that...
  f Despite the fact that...I still find ...
  g we were all very impressed by...

4 a iv b vii c ii d i e ix f x g vi

5 Possible answers
  a I would be grateful if you didn't play your car stereo so loudly when you come home at night. When the car is outside my house I can hear the music quite plainly and often it wakes up my daughter who starts crying. It can take me quite a while to get her back to sleep again, so please could you turn it down in future?
  b I wonder whether you remember that my graduation day is the 23rd of October; i.e. next month? As you gave me so much encouragement with my studies I would hate it if you weren't there to see me walk up on the stage. I do hope you can come!
  c I thoroughly enjoyed meeting you last week and talking over the simulator project that we will be working on together next year. I feel we have a good understanding of each other's area of business now and on behalf of our company, I would like to say that we look forward very much to working with you.
  d I'm so sorry that I forgot your birthday, especially when you not only remember mine, but also buy me such wonderful presents. In an effort to make up for my awful memory, I am enclosing tickets to the Shakespeare performance in Canterbury next month. I do hope you can go!

  e Once again, the garage door has been left unlocked, despite the fact that I have repeatedly asked you to make sure that you lock it when you arrive at work. If, one day, you find that your car or bicycle has been stolen, you will have only yourselves to blame. So please, lock up.
  f I'm just writing to say thanks very much for lending me your video camera. The family thoroughly enjoyed watching the film of the holiday and I've managed to print off some great pictures of the park animals.

6 Formal: a, c, e. Neutral: a, b (depending on relationship). Informal: b, d, f.

7 b This paragraph lays out the problem clearly and unemotionally. It sets the tone for the rest of the letter and is more likely to get a positive response.

8 a This paragraph is almost completely lifted from the question. It also contains too many ideas in one sentence.
  c This paragraph is muddled. It is trying to express too many ideas at once. Also, the word 'disgust' is too strong for the situation.

9 Sample answer
On 3rd May I purchased a 'Riteway' personal computer from your city store. The price of $2,500 included delivery and set up in my home. However, when it was delivered yesterday, the delivery man was quite unaware of the agreement and left without setting up the computer for me.

Obviously this is not what I was expecting. I had taken the day off work to be at home when it was delivered, and was planning to use the computer that afternoon to write an urgent report. Not only is this very irritating, but I feel it is false advertising to offer a service to attract customers, and then deny this later.

I now have a computer at home that is not functioning and I would like to know when you intend to send a technician to my house to install it. Please ring me to discuss this matter urgently, or I shall have no alternative but to return the computer to your store for a refund. I will also be in touch with the Consumers Association and Riteway Computers.

IELTS task page 89 sample answer

Dear Sir,	*Gives details of membership and payment.*
In September 2003, I joined your Sports and Social Club as a full-time student member. Since then I have paid the monthly membership fees by direct debit from my bank: Nationwide in Sanderson Avenue, Kinghill.	
I have thoroughly enjoyed my club membership as it has provided me with useful opportunities to meet up with other young people and to participate in a number of different social activities. I have also been fortunate enough to play in some of the inter-club tennis tournaments and have taken advantage of the various classes available such as Yoga and T'ai chi.	*Expresses appreciation of club.*
However, my studies are now coming to an end and as I will shortly be returning to my home country, possibly for good, I regret that I no longer wish to continue my membership.	*Explains reasons for leaving.*
I would be grateful, therefore, if you could confirm in writing that the monthly fee will no longer be deducted from my bank account.	*Closing sentence requests confirmation.*

Writing Unit 7

1 Personal happiness, relationships, work, wealth.
2 It clarifies what is meant by 'relationships with other people'.
3 E.g. health.
4 It is philosophical – there is no correct answer.
5 'What are the key factors in achieving personal happiness?'
6 Men and women, approach academic study, organisation, attitude, ambition, impact.
7 No, it is linked to academic study.
8 The words 'organisation', 'attitude' and 'ambition' could be used as paragraph topics.
9 No, any approach can be taken as long as it directly addresses the question.
10 Friends are important in life.
11 There aren't any.
12 It is very repetitive.

13 By developing the main idea using two or three supporting points, see sample paragraph below.

Friends play an important role in my life and I would have difficulty living without them. First, they support me in a number of ways: by providing advice when I need it and good company when I want to go out and enjoy myself. These are the aspects of friendship that are easy to define. Other aspects are less easy to explain but there is often a bond between friends that keeps them together. It results in some of the very strong features of friendship such as the ability to accept each other's faults and forgive certain behaviour that might otherwise be considered irritating.

14 The organisation of study.
15 Individual versus group.
16 Women agree principles.
17 Men work alone.
18 Time management.
19 Women realistic about time.
20 Men under-estimate.

Writing Unit 8

1 Main ideas are in bold and supporting points in italics.

I certainly agree that people who come up with new ideas; in other words those who 'invent' or 'discover' things are terribly important to society as a whole. However, I also think there is a role in society for good imitators.	*Introduction – responds to task and adds a further consideration.*
No one would deny that key individuals must be thanked for providing us with certain facilities that we use every day. *Where would we be, for example, without basic items such as the washing machine, the television and, more recently, the computer?* These items are now used so regularly that we tend to take them for granted.	*1st paragraph relates to the importance of those who invent consumer products.*
In fact, the society we live in today has become increasingly consumer-oriented, and *while it may be possible to constantly update and improve consumer goods, not everyone where I live can afford the prices of these innovations. Furthermore not everyone lives in an area that has accessibility to the latest models on the market.* **For this reason, there is a value to be placed on being able to provide good copies of expensive items.**	*2nd paragraph develops the idea that those who copy well have a role in society. This idea is linked to the previous paragraph.*
Having said that, certain innovations have a more serious impact on our lives than consumer goods and cannot easily be replicated. *Vital medicines like penicillin and vaccines against dangerous diseases also exist because people made continual efforts to develop them.* Scientific ideas such as these enable us to live longer and escape illness.	*3rd paragraph highlights a more important aspect of discovery that cannot be replicated easily.*
Undoubtedly, scientists and engineers work extremely hard to make life better for us. In some areas, their work adds comfort to our lives, and if people copy their ideas it helps a wider population to benefit from them. However, in other areas, their contribution is unique, cannot be copied and without it we would be unlikely to survive or move forward.	*Conclusion is a summary of the main points in the answer.*

2 Assists clear thinking.
3 Gives sense of pride in studies. } (in any order)
4 Reflects on staff.
5 What about businesses?
6 Does a home have to be clean? } (in any order)
7 Individual study areas.
8 Funding restrictions.
9 Staffing needs. } (in any order)
10 Cost of facilities.

11 a Introduction – the sentence implies that the writer is going to begin exploring the topic.
   b Conclusion – the writer is referring back to arguments that have been stated.
   c Conclusion – the writer's use of 'thus' indicates that previous arguments are being referred to.
   d Introduction – the writer's use of questions suggests that these ideas will be explored.

Possible answers
12 On the whole, it must be the case that a clean learning environment promotes good study habits.

13 At first glance, the statement seems reasonable but I wonder whether the condition of the learning environment has any effect on the way we study.
14 I certainly agree that it's good to study in pleasant surroundings; however, it's questionable whether these have any direct impact on the success of our studies.
15 The statement may be true but I think we have to question, first of all, what is meant by 'study well' and then whether this refers to the way we study or the overall success of our studies.
16 If the term 'environment' refers to the physical surroundings of a university, those that offer a pleasant learning environment should engender higher levels of motivation amongst students.

IELTS task page 95 sample answer

The idea that a marriage should be arranged by the parents of the couple, or by other members of the family, is quite acceptable to some societies, yet completely out of the question for others. It all depends on your cultural expectations.	*Introduces both systems.*
In so-called western societies, it is very unusual for marriages to be arranged. Most young people would not welcome the idea that their parents have the right to choose their partner for life. They feel that arranged marriages deny them their fundamental right to choose, even if they make a bad decision.	*Gives view against arranged marriages, supported by reasons.*
However, if we are honest about it, we might acknowledge that some parents organise their children's lives in such a way that they are likely to meet and marry partners the parents approve of. It could be said that this is, to some extent, similar to an arranged marriage. It is always better when families support the relationship and welcome the grandchildren.	*Concedes that many western marriages compare to arranged marriages. Supports both arrangements.*
People for whom arranged marriages are the cultural norm often argue that the likelihood of the marriage lasting is greater when it is set up in this manner. Parents can be assured that their children are joining a family of similar standing and cultural background, and this, in the long run, makes for a more stable society. If your parents' marriage was arranged, and has worked well, then why should you question the custom?	*Argues in favour of arranged marriages and supports the view.*
The important thing to ensure is that people are never forced into a marriage which will make them unhappy or lead to an unequal relationship where one partner is exploited by the other. This applies in all societies and situations.	*Concludes that both systems should result in happy marriages.*

Writing Unit 9

1 c **2** b **3** h **4** d **5** f **6** g **7** d **8** e **9** c **10** a
11 What crime is more shocking than cold-blooded murder?
12 Why would anyone want to go to prison?
13 Where are the crime rates higher than in the big cities?
14 How can you compare a crime in one country with the same crime in another?
15 Who can say how long someone should spend in prison?
16 We have a tendency to (simply) accept mobile phones regardless of the long-term effect (they may have) on our health.
17 In my view it is (totally) unethical for parents to (be able to) choose the sex of their baby.
18 Despite the fact that a lot of steps have been taken to help old people, we still don't do enough (for them).
19 I am doubtful whether many people really understand the impact of antibiotics.

20 There is little evidence to prove (the fact) that hamburgers are unhealthy.
21 I am always surprised when people say they prefer to work at home.

Possible answers
22 (In my view) fake designer watches work perfectly well.
23 Nowadays, young children tend to spend too much time playing computer games.
24 When will we realise that cutting down so many trees causes permanent damage to the environment?
25 Although some children's stories seem very frightening, children still (seem to) enjoy reading them.
26 I am unconvinced that teams work as effectively in business as individuals (do).
27 By 'fit' I mean having the capacity to do regular exercise.
28 It is not inconceivable that tourists will be able to...

29 It is not unusual/uncommon for children to be able to...
30 It is not impossible/inconceivable for/that women to be/might be able to...
31 It is not uncommon for well-established painters to decide to change...
32 Sample answer

Countries where fresh water has always been in scarce supply have long known the importance of conserving water. However, people in parts of the world where water is in plentiful supply are also starting to realise the importance of conserving water.	*Introduces idea of water conservation by comparing views in different parts of the world.*
Water is essential to life. Our bodies consist of 70% water and no living creature can go for more than a couple of days without drinking fresh water. We also use it to wash ourselves, to grow crops, for disposal of waste and for recreational purposes like swimming and sport.	*Main idea stated boldly and supported by examples.*
Despite this, there is a tendency to forget that water must be collected, cleaned and piped to our homes. This is an expensive and time-consuming business. In addition, in hot climates where water evaporates easily, it is doubtful whether storing it in open dams is at all efficient.	*Main idea of storage developed and a question posed.*
As individuals, there are various ways that we can use to help to save water; for example, by not running the tap unnecessarily when we brush our teeth or wash our dishes. Recycling is another answer. For instance, some people collect rain water from the roof and use it to water the garden. In this way, you not only reduce your consumption of water, but also use it more efficiently.	*Focus of main idea: individual responsibility, with examples to support.*
Above all, we should not forget the importance of water or waste it unnecessarily. Any kind of drought is always a reminder that we should never take our water for granted and that every drop counts.	*Conclusion reinforces main argument and ends with an appropriate expression.*

Writing Unit 10

1 By using *firstly, secondly, thirdly.*
2 Yes, as this is a list.
3 It reinforces the main idea.
4 By providing a clearer, more focused opening sentence.
By developing each of the supporting points.
By writing longer sentences with appropriate links within and between them.
By using a wider range of language.
5 By using a range of linkers.
6 *Actually, besides* and *on the other hand* are used incorrectly.
7 It repeats the main idea in the first sentence and so loses its impact.
8 By replacing the rhetorical question with a sentence that leads into the reasons being given.
By avoiding the repetition in the use of 'people'.
By developing the supporting points better – here the student really repeats the same point as part of the development, e.g. 'it would be very expensive to do this and some people can't afford it'.
By ending the paragraph better.
By using a wider range of language.
9 It relates the idea to research, those responsible and the task, and it sets a clear focus for the reader by referring to hotels.
10 It is rich, varied and precise.
11 Yes; e.g. *to begin with* is a useful alternative to *firstly.*
12 It means *in addition to*, and links the idea of the danger of the journey to the moon with the problem of survival in a different atmosphere.
13 To highlight the improbability (in her view) of ever being able to do this; it also adds a touch of humour.
14 There are opposite ideas here, so the student is likely to use a contrastive structure; the inclusion of pros and cons may also lead to some use of concessional structures or to the expression of doubt or the rejection of other arguments.
15 The impact on humans of seeing the Earth from such a distance.
16 By giving examples.
17 *Possible answer*
As far as I can see, there are both advantages and disadvantages to the development of moon holidays for the tourist. On the one hand, a moon holiday might seem attractive in that it would offer not only a unique holiday experience but also an unforgettable life experience. As films have repeatedly shown, our view of life on Earth is likely to be permanently altered by a trip to the moon.

On the other hand, there are various drawbacks to consider. For those who are concerned about access to important facilities such as hospitals or who rely on our telecommunications systems, the moon is unlikely to be an attractive tourist destination. Ultimately, isn't the moon just too far away? People are still reluctant to travel across the world; they are unlikely to want to hop on a space shuttle and venture into zero-gravity.

18 *Possible answer a*
I don't think 'moon holidays' are ever likely to be possible. The media frequently reports on things like the building of moon hotels and provides images of a typical moon holiday resort, but these are just speculative. You can construct and encapsulate an atmosphere on the moon that can sustain human life, but then you have to maintain it. Also you have to find people willing to work on the moon. There is also the problem of attracting sufficient numbers of tourists in order to make such a business financially viable. I think the obstacles to this type of project are simply too great for moon holidays to ever be a viable option.

Possible answer b – this is a better version of a.
I would question whether so-called 'moon holidays' are ever likely to be possible. Although the media frequently reports on things like the building of moon hotels and provides images of a typical moon holiday resort, I doubt whether these are anything more than speculative. Even if it is possible to construct and encapsulate an atmosphere on the moon that can sustain human life, how practical is it going to be to maintain this? Are those involved in the development of moon holidays ever likely to find people willing to work on the moon? That apart, there is also the problem of attracting sufficient numbers of tourists in order to make such a business financially viable. All in all, I think the obstacles to this type of project are simply too great for moon holidays to ever be a realistic option.

IELTS task page 103 sample answer

Holidays are important because they provide a break from our normal daily routine and from the world of work. Traditionally, holidays have been seen as a time for relaxation and as an opportunity to visit another country in order to find out about its geography and customs. Nowadays, however, it seems that other types of holiday are becoming popular.	*Introduces the idea of holidays and repeats the idea in the question, in the writer's own words.*
Some people want their holiday to be a kind of adventure, and find this more exciting than going to the beach or visiting museums. On an adventure holiday, you may stay in quite basic accommodation, rather than a luxurious hotel. Activities may involve things such as bush walking or cycling, or may form part of an aid project designed to help communities in remote areas. Holidays such as these are popular with people of all ages and can often help to promote tourism in rural environments.	*Introduces the main idea of 'adventure holiday' with explanation and further support.*
The increasing popularity of dangerous sports has also boosted the number of adventure holidays; for example, water sports, mountain climbing or paragliding. These holidays are more popular with the younger generation, as they can be both physically and mentally demanding. Participants are often seeking the sort of thrills that they cannot get in ordinary life.	*Further explores the topic of adventure holidays.*
There is now greater awareness of the damaging effects of mass tourism and this may be one reason for the changing nature of holidays. This can only be a good thing. But perhaps people are also discovering that it is just as refreshing to take an active holiday, as it is to lie on a beach – though that is still a question of personal preference.	*Sums up reasons for the changing nature of holidays.*

Writing Unit 11

Possible answers

1 Even though most people get nervous about giving a speech, they tend to lose their nerves once they get started.

2 I tend to disagree with the popular view that music is beneficial to children. While it's true that children like music, I wonder whether they need to learn it at school? It may even use up valuable time...

3 Libraries are marvellous places; however, they need to improve their image in that many people find them boring.

4 As a result of an effective anti-smoking campaign and the rising cost of cigarettes, smoking among young people has dropped by 2% over the last two years.

5 Global warming is a reality even though there is no real evidence of climatic change. In addition, changes in climate have been a feature of the Earth's history.

6 The market is rapidly expanding (or expanding rapidly).

7 Increasing numbers of women are going out to work.

8 This book is exceptionally good. *or* This book is exceptional.

9 I mistakenly bought the wrong size shoes.

10 People repeatedly argue (or argue repeatedly) that violence on television is harmful.

11 The number of people who work at home has increased threefold. OR There has been a threefold increase in...

12 Country A's exports are considerably higher than country B's.

Corrected answer
Young children go to school for a number of different reasons: not only to learn essential skills such as reading, writing and arithmetic, but also to learn how to get on with each other. In other words, the acquisition of social skills is equally important.

One of the most effective ways to teach young children how to work together is to get them to create music together, particularly music which involves percussion instruments such as drums and symbols, instruments which do not require a high level of skill to play and which children seem to enjoy enormously. Learning to play music together teaches them the important skill of co-operation which does not always come naturally to young children.

Children can be introduced to musical concepts like pitch and rhythm through a number of activities: dancing, singing and playing instruments are all appropriate and enjoyable. In this way they become familiar with music and, if well guided, go on to enjoy all kinds of music throughout the rest of their lives.

Speaking Unit 1

| **1** i | **2** g | **3** d | **4** a | **5** b |
| **6** c | **7** e | **8** f | **9** j | **10** h |

Guided speaking

Name of place	Melbourne / In state of Victoria
Location	Australia / S.E. Australia
Good points	Fine architecture, wide streets, trams, more elegant than Sydney / Grandfather was a tram driver / smarter clothes, better restaurants
Closing words	Hot summers, cold winters / Even have our own little penguins.

Speaking Unit 2

1 The boy
2 Boy – 1   Woman – 2   Girl – 2
3 Because her answer is slightly unexpected – not a direct answer like the boy.
4 To be honest with you = I'm going to give a very strong opinion. She also uses 'as far as I'm concerned' which is a forceful way of saying 'in my opinion'.

Guided speaking

Second speaker

Sport	Rowing / 8 in the boat
Tough things	Hard work / Blisters on hands / muscles ache / get up 4.30am
Good things	Good feeling / Sense of satisfaction
Closing words	The best thing ... is winning!

Speaking Unit 3

1 No – omits the time of the visit.
2 Yes – mentioned who she went with.
3 Present simple tense.
4 Because the speaker is mostly describing the zoo.
5 It's an excellent zoo.
6 Past simple tense.
7 Because the speaker is talking about an event in the past.
8 It was very exciting.

Speaking Unit 4

List of language features – not exhaustive
Fluency   a, c, h, i, j, l,
Vocabulary   b, i, o, p, q
Pronunciation   f, g, n,
Grammar & Accuracy   a, b, d, e, j, k, m,

1 This is a topic about something you might do in the future.
2 The tense will be predominantly conditional or present. The content of the talk will be drawn from your imagination rather than based on a past experience.

Speaking Unit 5

Assessing the question

1 Give a reason.
2 Explain something.
3 Make an assessment/Look ahead.
4 Give a reason.
5 Compare.
6 Give a reason / Explain something.

Speaking Unit 6

Sample questions

a How do you feel about the International Space Station? Do you think it's a useful project?
b We've been talking about the benefits of museums. Can you tell me what kind of museums you like going to?
c On the subject of girls and boys schooling, do you think mixed schools are better than single sex schools?
d Some people are against the idea of DNA testing as a way of tracking down criminals, because they say it represents a loss of privacy. Do you think it does?
e Adventure holidays have become very popular recently. Would you like to go on an adventure holiday?

1 Apparently we don't need another telephone line...
2 Frankly, I think the monarchy is completely out of date.
3 Personally, I am not in favour of sports like fox-hunting...
4 Apparently, / Regrettably, the bushfires were started deliberately...
5 Obviously, some people enjoy horror movies because otherwise...
6 Theoretically, it's easy to book a flight on the Internet ...
7 Regrettably, the days of the great passenger liners are gone.
8 Realistically, I don't think I can finish my degree in three years.
9 Hopefully, we will see a change in smoking habits...
10 Surely we don't have to buy another text book...
    i f **ii** b **iii** a **iv** e

Acknowledgements

The authors and publishers would like to thank the teachers and students who trialled and commented on the material:

Australia: Garry Adams, Peter Gray; Greece: Margaret Franey; Hong Kong: Wu Ruiling; New Zealand: Darren Conway; Portugal: Denise Beale; Taiwan: Danyal Freeman; UK: Jan Benjamin, Paul Bress, Sue Derry-Penz, Claire Gipson, Jane Sealy-Thompson, Susan Yates, Jane Richards; United Arab Emirates: Lynne Kennedy, Philip Lodge, Paul Rawcliffe

The authors and publishers are grateful to the following for permission to use copyright material in *Insight into IELTS Extra*. While every effort has been made, it has not been possible to identify the sources of all the material used and in such cases the publishers would welcome information from the copyright owners:

For the history of McDonalds on p. 15, © McDonald's Corporation; for pp. 21-22 derived from 'Gone Native' published in November 2001, reproduced with permission from *New Scientist Magazine*, the global authority on science and technology news © RBI www.NewScientist.com, *New Scientist Magazine*, November 2001 for p. 26 'We all have our image', *New Scientist*, November 2001, for p. 26 'How intelligent are you', *New Scientist*, November 2001 for p. 27 'Emma Darwin', *New Scientist*, May 2000, for the extract on p. 31 from Comic Relief, and for the extract on p. 31 from 'Why the internet is a house of cards', *New Scientist Magazine*, July 2000, *New Scientist Magazine*, May 2001, for the article and illustration on pp. 34-35, 'Fruitful drinking' by David Cohen, and for the article and illustration on p. 36, 'Time stands still' by Andy Coghlan, published July 2001; Adrian Tame for p. 24 'Life in orbit' published in the Herald Sun, Melbourne, 2001; *The Computing Teacher* Volume 20 No:1 for p. 28 derived from 'Computer Viruses', Copyright © 1992, ISTE (International Society for Technology in Education), 800.336.5191 (U.S.& Canada) or 541.302.3777 (Int'l), iste@iste.org, www.iste.org all rights reserved; the extract on p. 30 from "Time" Microsoft ® Encarta® Encyclopaedia CD Microsoft Corporation, all rights reserved; *Scientific American* for the extract on p. 30 'Animating Human Motion' by Jessica K. Hodgins, March 1998, *Scientific American* for the article on pp. 52-53 'Do apes ape?' by Andrew Whiten and Christophe Boesch, 2000, reprinted with permission. Copyright © Scientific American, Inc. All rights reserved; Marc Bekoff for the extract on p. 31 'The essential joys of play', published in the *BBC Wildlife Magazine*, August 2000; *Focus Magazine* June 1998, for the article on p. 31 'Our home and beyond' by Sally Palmer, and for the pie chart on p. 71, 'Athlete's dietary requirements', Focus April 2001, for the diagram on p. 81 'Hawaiian chain', *Focus* July 2001; Jeanette Hyde for the article on p. 32, 'Cutting corners on the world', first published in *The Times*, 5 December 1998; Michael Legat for the extract from 'Writers' rostrum' on p. 38, first published in *Writing*

Magazine, June-July 2001; *The Economist*, 10 March 2001, for the extract on p. 39 from 'The sky's the limit', by Iain Carson, and for the extract on p. 43 from 'Thunderclouds and flying tigers', *The Economist*, 22 July 2000, and the article on p. 45 'Behind the scenes at the museum', from *The Economist*, 23 December 2000, and for the article on pp. 55-56 'Fingering fingerprints', from *The Economist*, 16 December 2000, and for the graph on p. 70 'Move over, China', *The Economist*, 31 March 2001, for the graph on p. 71 'Selling fewer, making more' *Economist*, 31 March 2001, the graph on p. 71 'Where's the Doc?', *Economist*, 1 September 2001, and the graph on p. 72 'We're talking telephone numbers', *The Economist*, 15 September 2001, for the graph on p. 73 'Hoop dreams', *The Economist*, 28 April 2001, and for the graph on p. 74 'A degree of progress', *The Economist*, 16 December 2000, for the graph on p. 75 'Slowing up', *Economist*, 4 August 2001, and for the graph on p. 78 'Mexico's imports', *The Economist*, 25 August 2001; Charles Jonscher for the extract on p. 44 from *Wired Life* published by Bantam Press. Used by permission of Transworld Publishers, a division of The Random House Group Limited. (Copyright © Charles Jonscher 1999) by permission of PFD on behalf of Dr Charles Jonscher; Sarah Perrin for the article on pp. 48-49 'Soft centres, hard profits', first published in *Accountancy*, April 1998; the Picasso Museum, Antibes for the extract on p. 60 from their information guide; the extract on p. 60 from the museum guide, courtesy Australian National Maritime Museum, Sydney; the Government of Western Australia - Fremantle Prison for the extract on p. 61 from the visitor's guide; *The Guardian*, 22 July 1997, for the article on p. 67 'World's top languages' by John Carvel, © The Guardian , and for the graph on p. 44 'Changing voices', from *The Guardian*, 6 May 1997, © The Guardian, and for the graph on p. 53 'Demand for electricity' from *The Guardian*, 18 October 1994, © The Guardian; *The Sydney Herald*, 19 January 2001, for the graph on p. 77 'What those kids are doing', reproduced with the permission of John Fairfax Holdings Limited. All rights reserved, the article may not be published, broadcast or redistributed in any form; *Geographical Magazine*, May 2000, for the diagram on p. 81 'Hawaiian chain' by Norman Millers; *The Times*, 4 January 2002, for the diagram and map of the Eiffel Tower on p. 83, © Times Newspapers Limited 2002.

The Publishers are grateful to the following for permission to include photographs:

Ardea London/François Cohier for p.45; Adrian Warren for p.52; Gareth Boden Photography for p.121; Flight International Collection/Simon Everett for p.39; The Guide Dogs for the Blind Association for p.14; MacDonalds for p.15(t); Metropolitan Police for p.55; Paul Mulcahy for p.15(b), p.48, p.71; Science Photo Library for p.27; NASA for p.24; Still Pictures/Hjalte Tin for p.36.

Picture research by Valerie Mulcahy